Man and Salvation in Literature

Charles Moeller

MAN

AND

SALVATION

IN

LITERATURE

Translated by

Charles Underhill Quinn

UNIVERSITY OF NOTRE DAME PRESS
NOTRE DAME   LONDON

Copyright © 1970 by
University of Notre Dame Press
Notre Dame, Indiana 46556

Published as *L'Homme moderne devant le salut*,
© 1965, by Les Éditions Ouvrières, Paris

Library of Congress Catalog Card Number: 77-122048
Manufactured in the United States of America by
NAPCO Graphic Arts, Inc., Milwaukee, Wisconsin

Acknowledgments

GRATEFUL ACKNOWLEDGMENT IS MADE FOR EXCERPTS FROM THE following works:

Acquainted With the Night, by Heinrich Böll, translated by Richard Graves. Copyright 1954 by Henry Holt. Reprinted by permission of Joan Daves.

Diary 1923–1957 by Julian Green, selected by Kurt Wolff and translated by Anne Green, reprinted by permission of the American publisher: Harcourt, Brace & World, Inc.

"History and Politics" in *The Collected Works of Paul Valéry,* edited by Jackson Mathews, translated by Denise Folliot, Bollingen Series XLV (Copyright © 1962 by Bollingen Foundation). Reprinted by permission of Princeton University Press.

Memoirs of a Dutiful Daughter by Simone de Beauvoir, reprinted by permission of The World Publishing Company. Copyright © 1959 by Simone de Beauvoir.

The Fall and Exile and the Kingdom by Albert Camus, translated by Justin O'Brien, reprinted by permission of Random House, Inc., and Alfred A. Knopf, Inc.

Jean Barois by Roger Martin du Gard, translated by Stuart Gilbert. Copyright 1949 by The Viking Press, Inc. Reprinted by permission of The Viking Press, Inc.

Hiroshima mon amour by Marguerite Duras, translated by Richard Seaver. Copyright © 1961 by Grove Press, Inc. Reprinted by permission of Grove Press, Inc.

v

The Condemned of Altona, by Jean-Paul Sartre, translated by Sylvia and George Leeson, reprinted by permission of Random House, Inc. and Alfred A. Knopf, Inc.

Dearest Father by Franz Kafka, copyright © 1954 by Schocken Books, Inc.

Diaries: 1914–1923 by Franz Kafka, copyright © 1949 by Schocken Books, Inc.

The Two Sources of Morality and Religion by Henri Bergson. Translation by R. Ashley Audra and Cloudesley Brereton with the assistance of W. Horsfall Carter. Copyright 1935, © 1963 by Holt, Rinehart and Winston, Inc. Reprinted by permission of Holt, Rinehart and Winston, Inc.

Eloges and Other Poems by St.-John Perse, translated by Louise Varèse, Bollingen Series LV (Copyright © 1956 by Bollingen Foundation). Reprinted by permission of Princeton University Press.

Anabasis by St.-John Perse, translated by T. S. Eliot, reprinted by permission of the American publishers: Harcourt, Brace & World, Inc.

Winds by St.-John Perse, translated by Hugh Chisholm, Bollingen Series XXXIV, 2nd edition, 1961 (Copyright © 1953 by Bollingen Foundation). Reprinted by permission of Princeton University Press.

Seamarks by St.-John Perse, translated by Wallace Fowlie, Bollingen Series LXVII (Copyright © 1958 by Bollingen Foundation). Reprinted by permission of Princeton University Press.

Chronique by St.-John Perse, translated by Robert Fitzgerald, Bollingen Series LXIX (Copyright © 1961 by Bollingen Foundation). Reprinted by permission of Princeton University Press.

Vipers' Tangle by François Mauriac, published by Sheed & Ward, Inc., New York. Reprinted by permission of the publisher.

Each in His Darkness, by Julian Green, translated by Anne Green. Copyright © 1961 by William Heinemann Ltd. and Pantheon Books. Reprinted by permission of Pantheon Books, a division of Random House, Inc.

The Diary of a Country Priest by Georges Bernanos. Copyright 1937 by The Macmillan Company, renewed 1965 by The Macmillan Company. Reprinted by permission of The Macmillan Company.

"The Hollow Men" in Collected Poems 1909–1962 by T. S. Eliot, copyright, 1936, by Harcourt, Brace & World, Inc.; copyright, © 1963, 1964, by T. S. Eliot. Reprinted by permission of the publisher.

Murder in the Cathedral by T. S. Eliot, copyright, 1935, by Harcourt, Brace & World, Inc.; renewed, 1963, by T. S. Eliot. Reprinted by permission of the publishers.

The Cocktail Party, copyright, 1950, by T. S. Eliot. Reprinted by permission of Harcourt, Brace & World, Inc.

The Elder Statesman by T. S. Eliot, reprinted with the permission of Farrar, Straus & Giroux, Inc. Copyright © 1959 by Thomas Stearns Eliot.

The Wild Orchid by Sigrid Undset, translated by Arthur G. Chater, reprinted by permission of the American publisher, Alfred A. Knopf, Inc.

The Burning Bush by Sigrid Undset, translated by Arthur G. Chater, reprinted by permission of the American publisher, Alfred A. Knopf, Inc.

Kristin Lavransdatter, by Sigrid Undset, translated by Charles Archer, reprinted by permission of the American publisher, Alfred A. Knopf, Inc.

The Master of Hestviken, by Sigrid Undset, translated by Arthur G. Chater, reprinted by permission of the American publisher, Alfred A. Knopf, Inc.

The Mystery of the Charity of Joan of Arc by Charles Péguy, translated by Julian Green, copyright 1950, reprinted by permission of Pantheon Books, a division of Random House, Inc.

Tete d'Or by Paul Claudel, translated by J. S. Newberry. Reprinted by permission of Mercure de France.

The Satin Slipper by Paul Claudel, in the translation of Rev. John O'Connor, published by Sheed & Ward, Inc., New York.

Contents

Acknowledgments   v

Preface   xi

PART ONE

STEPPING-STONES AND OBSTACLES

1. Salvation Literature and the Literature of Happiness	3
2. Pluralism and Christianity	9
3. Salvation as an Objective Fact	17
4. Salvation as Subjective	63

PART TWO

POSITIVE APPROACHES

5. A Bridge Writer: St.-John Perse	81
6. Personal Salvation	97
7. Salvation of the Universe	118

Conclusion   185

Index   187

Preface

SALVATION IS A TERM COMMON TO ALL RELIGIONS AND EXPRESSES the hope of mankind. The Hebrew root word carries with it the ideas of expansion and rescue. Its basic experience is one of danger, where man risks his own destruction. For Israel, God alone is the "Rock of salvation" (Deut. 32:15). It is he alone who will give happiness in the messianic kingdom where righteousness and equity shall prevail. Out of a land of darkness the whole people is called to the promised land of light and everlasting life (Isa. 45:15) in the "new creation" (Isa. 41:20). There is but one saving answer to this call: faith, the burning hope of the salvation to come, since what God has made is the first fruit of salvation. Only the humble, those with a contrite heart, can call Yahweh their Savior (Ps. 34:18).

By delivering us from sin—which is a total death—Jesus has brought us salvation (Luke 1:77). Salvation is life. To be saved is to be transported from the kingdom of death to the kingdom of life, for salvation is *the risen Jesus.* His resurrected life saves us. Of course, only in hope are we saved (Rom. 8:24; Heb. 1:14, etc.), but this hope does not deceive us "because God's love has been poured into our hearts through the Holy Spirit which has been given to us" (Rom. 5:5).[1]

In the expansion and rescue of a people that believes in the everlasting life which Jesus gives those who repent of their sin, in their expansion into the kingdom of righteousness and equity, a new creation where we shall reign with Christ (2 Tim. 2:12), we have a reality that goes far beyond the notion of merely having one's own soul to save.

Because of their content, literary approximations remain only too human. Theological references will appear peripheral. Some elements will seem to be overemphasized, while others that stand out shining at the zenith of the Bible will appear to be underemphasized. The point of view chosen, on the border of theology and literature, leaves us open to converging attacks from literary critics who will be looking here for literature and theologians seeking theology. But these literary approximations may allow us to travel some distance along with those harried and crushed brothers of ours, the early morning suburban commuters. The reflection of salvation in these somewhat murky waters will undoubtedly lack the clarity of a mathematical diagram. But it has movement, and movement is life.

What follows originated in a series of conferences given to nuns at Champrosay in September of 1961. It is due to the attentiveness of the audience, the dedication of the secretary, Mlle. Manespa, and the kind assistance of Canon Paul Barrau that these originally quite disjointed notes have become a book.

"After two thousand years, it is perhaps today that we are most ready to listen to the words: 'Love one another,' and to live them, impregnated as they are with the immense joy of creation, in their universal plenitude."[2]

C.M.

---

[1] The first two paragraphs sum up the article "Attente du salut" in the *Dictionnaire encyclopédique de la Bible* (Paris: Turnout, 1960) and "Salut" in *Vocabulaire de théologie biblique* (Paris, 1962).

[2] P. Teilhard de Chardin, *Lettre de Pékin*, Christmas, 1943.

PART ONE

STEPPING-STONES
AND OBSTACLES

I

Salvation Literature and

The Literature of Happiness

WHAT DOES SALVATION REPRESENT IN THE EYES OF MODERN MAN, at least of a certain type of modern man? This is the question we shall attempt to answer.

It will not be possible to touch upon every aspect of this problem. We shall take our inspiration from literature even though this point of view may be incomplete. A woman novelist said to me recently: "I have the impression that the novel is less and less a means of communicating ideas or a world outlook. For modern man, the man in the street, the cinema and the song represent a much more important element in his sensibilities." No doubt, but literature is none the worse for it!

André Rousseaux[1] makes a distinction between the literature of happiness and the literature of salvation.

Montaigne, for example, is a representative of the literature of happiness. It tries to show man how he can create a happier life for himself. Cicero explained that study ought to make us *humaniores*, more human, more cultivated, with more delicate sensibilities. In other words this kind of literature supposes the house to be already built. We are the owners and we live in it. Shall we hang draperies of a single color or should they be different? Where shall we put the paintings? What style should we choose for the furniture?

With its intention of making man more human, the literature of happiness supposes that he is *already* human. It wants to

3

embellish and improve his life. The literature of salvation is its
antithesis: the house is burning or threatens to burn. There is
no longer any question of hanging draperies of this or that
color, or of choosing between Louis XV or Louis XVI furniture. We have to call the fire department and try to save the
essentials. Translated into somewhat less metaphorical language,
it is this. Man finds himself in a concrete situation about which
he is apprehensive. He lives under the sign of threats and
danger. He is faced with obstacles. Prior to all others, his basic
problem is one of knowing whether it is still possible to be
purely and simply "human," still possible to live a human life.

If it is true in the world that two men out of three do not
possess the barest minimum necessary for living a simply human
life, if, as Péguy said, they are not poor but destitute, living in
permanent anguish about tomorrow's bread, tomorrow's work,
then human life has come to a stage that is subhuman. The man
who lives is haunted by survival. The literature of salvation takes
its starting point from an awareness of this situation. This was
Sartre's point in his book: *Qu'est-ce que la littérature?* It is interesting to compare it to a book of the same title written by
Charles Du Bos. It dates from 1938[2] and Sartre's from 1948–49.

For Charles Du Bos literature is destined to express life
when life becomes aware of itself. According to Keats, life is
the "Vale of Soul-making." The soul is the inner life, the place
inhabited by the God who is both internal and eternal to
ourselves. Du Bos says:

> Literature is nothing but life itself when it is joined to full-
> ness of expression in a man of genius. . . . Without life,
> literature would have no content; but without literature life
> would be only a waterfall, a constant waterfall beneath which
> so many of us are submerged, a senseless waterfall that we are
> content to put up with, that we are incapable of understand-
> ing. In relation to this waterfall literature plays the role of a
> hydraulic system, draining off, catching, transporting and rais-
> ing the waters. . . . Literature has its beginnings in the soul,
> it is to our soul that it is addressed, and it will never truly
> encounter it unless our soul first responds to it with emo-
> tion. . . . Its true goal is that everything best about the world

become consubstantial with our soul, help it to grow, mature, be fulfilled, and lead it towards its own perfection. . . . Within the context of its participation in Christ, life, as it is in itself, has never been given a truer and deeper definition than what Keats said of it in a letter on the 15th of April, 1819: "Call the world, if you please, the Vale of Soul-making." Do you not see how necessary it is that a world of cares and sufferings exist in order that the intelligence be put to the test and be made into a soul?[3]

For Jean-Paul Sartre, literature's purpose is to unmask human beings, in their particular "situation" of "ensnared freedoms."

Literature's subject has always been man in the world . . . . It is really about the totality of mankind that a writer should write. Not about an abstract man who could exist in any age and for the timeless reader, but about the man of his own time and for his contemporaries. . . . Since no aristocrat's pride compels him now to deny that he is in a situation, he no longer seeks to go beyond his own time and testify about it for eternity; but since the situation is universal, he will express the hopes and the angers of all men, and by doing so, will give total expression of himself, not as a meta-physical creature, in the style of the medieval cleric, nor as a psychological animal, in the manner of the classics, nor even as a social entity, but as a totality emerging from the world in the void, enclosing in this totality all these struc-tures within the indissoluble unity of the human condition; literature is truly anthropological in the full sense of the word. . . . Whether he claims to speak for the Good and for divine Perfection, for the Beautiful or the True, a cler-icalist is always on the side of the oppressors. Watch-dog or clown: the choice is his. M. Benda chose empty chatter and M. Marcel the kennel; it is their right, but if one day literature is to be able to have its own essence, the writer— without class, without colleagues, without a salon, without an excess of honors, without indignity—will be thrown into the world, among men, and the very notion of clericalness will seem inconceivable. Moreover, the spiritual always depends upon an ideology and ideologies are liberties when they come about on their own, oppression when they are created. . . . The writer will know that his concern is not the adoration of the spiritual, but spiritualization. Spiritualization means a *new start*. And there is nothing to spiritualize, nothing to start anew except this multicolored and concrete world, with its awkwardness, its opaqueness, its zones of generality and its swarms of anecdotes, and this invincible Evil that gnaws away at it without ever being able to destroy it. The writer will take it up as it is, sweating, stinking, and monotonous, in order to introduce it to freedoms on the foundation of one freedom.[4]

The literature of salvation is marked by the anguish of not being able to live a human life. A man is cooped up in a crowded conglomeration of dwelling places that are too small, and he can never find the solitude and the silence necessary for a couple's privacy. This is the theme of a novel of Heinrich Böll: *Acquainted with the Night*.

He is describing for us the Germany of 1947. Three quarters of the houses were destroyed. People had to live on top of one another. Bogner has left home because he was living in one room with his wife and three children. They were aware of everything that was going on with their neighbors, who also heard everything. In such a life, where people who love one another can't have even the minimum of solitude, recollection or family privacy, men can never know the totality of love.

Alone in her wretched apartment, Bogner's wife says:

Whenever I move the cupboard away from the wall pieces of plaster flake off and fall on the floor between the feet of the cupboard whence they spread all over the room in a tide of chalky fragments. . . . The gritty dust grates under my feet and I hear the little boy coughing in his cubicle from inhaling the beastly stuff. I feel despair like some bodily pain. Fear gathers in my throat like a swelling which I try to swallow down. . . .

I have turned on the tap again and now I see myself in the depths of the glass and look with astonishment at my smiling face—the face of a stranger—as I listen to the rising note of the water running into the pail. I try in vain to recall my glance from the world behind the mirror and focus it on my own, my real face on which I know there is no smile.

In the far distance I see women, yellow-skinned women, washing their linen in slow-flowing streams and singing the while. I see black women digging in the crumbly earth. I hear the meaningless but fascinating drumming of idle men in the background. I see brown women treading the corn in stone troughs with their babies on their backs, while their men squat stupidly round a fire with their pipes in their mouths. And I see my white sisters in the tenement houses of London, New York, or Berlin, or in the dark alleys of the slums of Paris. I see their bitter faces listening in dread for a drunkard's shout. And far back in the mirror I see the hateful army advancing—the unknown, unsung hosts of vermin mobilizing to kill my children.[5]

What can fidelity still mean for this man and woman? Absolutely nothing, because they are in a situation that does not allow them to understand. Undoubtedly we ought not to conclude from this that the temporal situation ought to be changed before proclaiming the Gospel. I merely pose the problem without seeking to resolve it. Sociologists would have much to say, as well as doctors, lawyers and others. But each one of us as well, for "no man is an island." We may die alone, but we still live together.

NOTES TO CHAPTER 1

1. André Rousseaux, a French critic who was a longtime collaborator of the weekly, *Le Figaro littéraire*. He is the author of several books of criticism, such as *Littérature du XXᵉ siècle*. Luc Estang took up this theme in his remarkable novel: *Le Bonheur et le Salut*.

He underlines the frequent disparity between earthly happiness and the salvation given by grace.

2. These were courses given by Charles Du Bos in the United States.

3. Charles Du Bos, *Approximations*, VIII (Corréa, 1937), pp. 321, 324, 326, 320. Cf. also *Qu'est-ce que la littérature?* (Paris: Plon, 1945), pp. 10–11.

4. Jean–Paul Sartre, *Situations*, II (Paris: © Editions Gallimard, 1948), pp. 194–196.

5. Heinrich Böll, *Acquainted with the Night*, trans. Richard Graves (New York: Holt, 1954), pp. 45–46, 48–49. This is the English translation of *Und sagte kein einziges Wort*.

2

Pluralism and Christianity

IF THE "BURNING HOUSE" THEME HAS RECENTLY BEGUN TO DIS-
appear, at least in France, and in a part of modern English
literature, it has passed over into the cinema and the song.
It might be thought that this situation is ideal for the problem
of salvation. Salvation consists of announcing to men threatened
with death—a rather simple and basic notion—that they will not
die and will be saved. There is a possible harmony between
these men in danger and a salvation-oriented world vision. Yet
this notion is bereft of substance for many men, as for example
those nine-tenths of mankind who, with tired bodies and empty
minds, come out of factories and offices and rush into the
crushing aisles and compartments of subways. It is hard for us
to put ourselves in their place, to enter into communication
with them; the words we use no longer speak to them.

I. NO MUTUAL UNDERSTANDING

How is it that man is rediscovering the human condition under
the sign of menace and death, and that, at the same time the
notion of salvation awakens nothing in his heart? This is due
in large measure to vocabulary. I know a woman novelist who
is no longer a believer. Yet she does not fit into any of the
three categories of atheists that I was told about in my youth.
God's existence had been so well proven to me that I wondered
how there still could be atheists. Either they were not intelligent or else they just did not reflect (as if we always reflected!),

or else they did not think about it (it is the Pascalian pastime, in the style of Françoise Sagan, who once said to a reporter: "God! I never think of it!").[1] Later, I discovered that it is not possible to classify atheists according to the three categories. There are atheists in good faith who have loyally sought but have not found. From what I know about her and from her novels that I have read, this novelist is among these. In listening to what she said to me about the love that we live either on the level of daily reality or of dreams, which at certain times appear to be reality, I discovered values that can be integrated into a Christian world vision. I spoke to her about it, and may have awakened echoes of it within her. But had I wanted to convert her, I would have failed. The whole procedure was as if we were separated from each other by a wall of glass and spoke a different vocabulary. We were speaking of Teilhard de Chardin and she told me: "I have read him. I also had my husband read him. I went to a lecture given by a Belgian Jesuit who knew Teilhard de Chardin very well. I was profoundly amazed at the breadth with which he spoke of all that. He seemed to be saying that there was a way of integrating Teilhard de Chardin's ideas into a Christian vision of things." And she added this: "He is the only Christian writer who brings me out of my dark night."

A few quotes from Teilhard illustrate this attitude quite well.

In our day, for want of renewing their anxiety at a contact with reality, many believers allow a veil of conventional solutions to spread over the mysteries of life. And the scientists, lost in their minute research, or involved in a false materialism, seem not to see how to pose the basic question of the Future, even in the light of their own conquests, in the face of our activities. Drowned in the words they have created, Men risk losing sight of the problem to the point of no longer grasping the sense of what their own experiences have uncovered. Relying upon what Religion and Science have taught me for fifty years, I have sought here to to emerge. I have wanted to come out of the fog in order to find the view of things themselves.[2]

In his response to a survey made by *Esprit* in 1946, Teilhard said: "If I judge by myself, the great temptation of the century is (and will be increasingly more so) to find the world of Life and of Human Effort greater, closer, more mysterious and more alive than the God of Scripture."[3]

There are, then, real values in modern culture. Many atheists believe they must deny God in order to safeguard them. Perhaps they are in the process of discovering a God who is "more worthy of God," more "God." They are "feeling after" him, as St. Paul said.[4] But communications have to be set up. It is a question of vocabulary, of translation.

We are ill able to imagine to what extent the Church is isolated in the modern world, to what extent the words of the Pope reach non-believers only to the degree that they touch upon problems of general order, as for example John XXIII's encyclical *Pacem in Terris*. As a whole, very little of what the Popes say, and often in a very deformed fashion, passes from the Christian to the non-Christian world. This is an extremely important point and we shall have occasion to return to it when we examine the work of Gertrud von Le Fort.

II. THE INSULARITY OF CHRISTIANITY

We have just seen the importance of vocabulary renewal. To this must be added the fact of the Church's insularity in a pluralistic world. From the perspective of the City of God, the whole world is Christian, has heard speak of Christ, and knows the Christian law. How then is it possible that men to whom we speak of salvation remain deaf to what we say, while they acknowledge that they are in danger of death, in danger of leading a life unworthy of a human being?

If on the other hand we put ourselves in a diaspora perspective,[5]—the dispersion of the people of God in a divided world— the problem of unbelief becomes comprehensible. The sign of God, the sign of God's salvation is necessarily veiled, for when God reveals himself he can do so only as the "hidden God." As Pascal has told us, "God is sufficiently revealed in the Scriptures for those who truly seek him, and they find him. God is sufficiently hidden in the Scriptures for those who do not seek him with all their heart, and they do not find him." However, a second veil covers the first, since we live in "a world where doubt has become the general opinion." For Julian Green we live in a society where what is self-evident is no longer faith but differing opinions about faith. The astonishing thing is that a person believes, while in the view of medieval Christendom it was astonishing that a person did not believe:

> Asked Father Couturier the other day if he had ever thought about the happiness of medieval men who lived in a world with so little room for doubt and where, generally speaking, everybody believed in the same thing. But all of us who live in a world where doubt is, to a certain extent, the general opinion, how can we not feel isolated and like lost children in modern civilization, we and our singular ideas about the incarnation and the transubstantiation (singular in the eyes of the world, but as natural to us as the sun in the sky)? . . . the first Christians, lost amidst Roman civilization, must have felt a little the way we feel today.[6]

In 1942 he remarked:

> The State of Christianity in 1942: English children "evacuated" from the coast inland are questioned by grownups. The latter ask them who is Christ. Answer: A swear word. That is all they know about him. All they know of Christ is this blasphemed name. The real causes of the war are perhaps to be found in facts like these.[7]

Four days later he added:

> I thought with sorrow about all the ground lost by the Church. She will not die since Christ has said that the gates of hell will not prevail against her, but it is possible that the day may come where the truth will be represented only by a few thousand persecuted Catholics, having at their head a little old man in a white cassock who will be hidden away in some catacomb. "When the Son of Man returns to earth, do you think he will find faith there?"[8]

In this perspective, we understand that someone born outside of Christianity, either because he was never baptized or because he received merely a folksy Christianity, may feel like a stranger to "salvation." For such a person the "great sign raised up among the nations" is doubly veiled. This is not a situation proper to our own age. We are simply more aware of it. Theologians are beginning to integrate this fact in their apologetics. We are in a world divided not only as a consequence of hatred but also because of differing world visions, each of which is looked upon as total. Paul Valéry mentioned this as early as 1919 in a famous passage:

And what made the disorder in the mind of Europe? The free coexistence, in all her cultivated minds, of the most dissimilar ideas, the most contradictory principles of life and learning. That is characteristic of a *modern* epoch. . . .

Well then! Europe in 1914 had perhaps reached the limit of modernism in this sense. Every mind of any scope was a crossroads for all shades of opinion; every thinker was an international exposition of thought. . . . How much material wealth, how much labor and planning it took, how many centuries were ransacked, how many heterogeneous lives were combined, to make possible such a carnival, and to set it up as the supreme wisdom and the triumph of humanity? . . .

Standing, now, on an immense sort of terrace of Elsinore that stretches from Basel to Cologne, bordered by the sands of Nieuport, the marshes of the Somme, the limestone of Champagne, the granites of Alsace . . . our Hamlet of Europe is watching millions of ghosts.

But he is an intellectual Hamlet, meditating on the life and death of truths; for ghosts, he has all the subjects of our controversies; for remorse, all the titles of our fame. He is bowed under the weight of all the discoveries and varieties of knowledge, incapable of resuming this endless activity; he broods on the tedium of rehearsing the past and the folly of always trying to innovate. He staggers between two abysses—for two dangers never cease threatening the world: order and disorder.

Every skull he picks up is an illustrious skull. *Whose was it?* This one was *Lionardo*. . . . And that other skull was *Leibnitz*, who dreamed of universal peace. And this one was *Kant* . . . and *Kant begat Hegel, and Hegel begat Marx, and Marx begat*. . . .

"Farewell, ghosts! The world no longer needs you—or me. By giving the name of progress to its own tendency to a fatal precision, the world is seeking to add to the benefits of life the advantages of death. A certain confusion still reigns; but in a little while all will be made clear, and we shall witness at last the miracle of an animal society, the perfect and ultimate anthill."[9]

Of course, in France and Belgium we still live in a basically Christian world. But in the United States this is no longer true. It is hard to sit down in an airplane seat or to take one's place in a cafeteria without one's neighbor introducing himself and telling you how much money he makes a week. Often he will also speak of religion. When I would say I was a Catholic priest he was interested. But he would have been just as interested if I had told him I was a Mormon. In this climate, the word *salvation* awakens a certain interest, but the notion of *Christian* salvation is lost amid the din of differing opinions.

There is a temptation to see this as a haughty refusal. Surely, if God is God, if he revealed himself through Christ, this call implies a change in attitude, a conversion. There is an element of freedom in adherence, a gift of self of which one should be aware. Yet we should suspect bad faith only in the last analysis. In this area we may never give a definitive judgment, since only God will be the judge: "*Ego retribuam* . . . I shall make judgment."

During a time I spent in Canada, among my pupils I had a young English Canadian couple. After the course the husband introduced himself: "I am from an Anglican family, but I no longer have the faith. I no longer believe in anything. What you said about literature presented within a Christian perspective is bewildering. Never has a university professor thought of presenting literature in that fashion. In the English-speaking world it is absolutely unheard of to speak as you speak. Still, I am very enthusiastic about it." I remember one day when he told me about the hostility felt by an English Canadian, faithful to the Crown, toward the Catholic French Canadians. I found what he had to say painful, but he had to speak. Toward the end of the day he asked me: "Essentially, Father, what is the kernel of Christianity for you?" I thought for a moment and then answered: "You said yourself that you dislike the modern world, you find it inhuman and impersonal, but that because of your wife, for her and with her, you are able to bear it, accept it and agree to do something in it. Then you added that you would never love your wife as she deserved. You said again that when you were separated from her, it did not disturb you, since she was present to you and you would love her more afterward. Fine. It is perfectly possible to integrate all of this within a perspective of love." He insisted: "But what does your God add to it?" I then replied: "He gives a meaning to your love. If ever you are separated definitively from your wife, either because she is sick or has died, or because your love is threatened in some way, your love will still continue to have meaning. Basically, Christianity gives meaning to human pain by faith in the resurrection." He answered: "I had never given it a thought!"

This made me understand the extent to which we use a vocabulary that does not "come across," or only with difficulty. It is, furthermore, a vocabulary that is quite far from that of the Bible.

NOTES TO CHAPTER 2

1. A play on words. The French phrase is: *Dieu! je n'y pense jamais*, and it may mean either "My God! I never think about it," or "God? I never think of him."

2. P. Teilhard de Chardin, *Oeuvres*, VI (Paris: Ed. du Seuil, 1962), p. 25. The text dates from 1931.

3. *Esprit*, no. 125, p. 254.

4. Acts 17:27.

5. *Diaspora*: the situation in which the Church is a minority in a world where the majority is not Christian.

6. Julian Green, *Diary 1928–1957*, sel. by Kurt Wolff, trans. by Anne Green (New York: Harcourt, 1964), p. 159.

7. *Ibid.*, p. 124.

8. Julian Green, *Journal*, III (Paris: Librairie Plon, 1946), pp. 205–206.

9. Paul Valéry, *History and Politics*, ed. Jackson Mathews, trans. Denise Folliot, in *The Collected Works of Paul Valéry*, X, Bollingen Series XLV (New York: Bollingen Foundation, 1962), pp. 27–30.

3

Salvation as an Objective Fact

YOU KNOW THE ANECDOTE ABOUT THE ASSIGNMENT TO WRITE A
dissertation on the camel, where the German made a distinction
between the "subjective" camel and the "objective" camel. This
is the kind of distinction I am about to make.

Objectively, modern man is attracted by three aspects of
"salvation": justice, life, and love; ultimately an awareness of
responsibility that may go as far as a feeling of guilt.

From the subjective viewpoint, we must point out initially that
the notion of salvation, as we shall use it in our attempt at unrav-
eling our very extensive problem, implies a gift that God alone
can give. It is a grace, a call to which we respond. Our response
is made in grace, through it and with it. For modern man every
response is problematical, for man "has to fend for himself," he
must act, and transform the world by creating values.

I. JUSTICE

Salvation is first of all justice. Two out of three men in the world
are lacking the minimum necessary for life. Many, even Christians, feel that God is ineffectual. Salvation does not bring about
justice on earth. Surely, the Kingdom of God is not of this world,
but it has to begin in this world. All who have taken seriously
grace and the love of God and of men have brought about a
beginning here on earth of that justice which is one of the
attributes of God in the Bible. St. Vincent de Paul, St. Catherine
of Genoa, St. John Bosco found solutions where everyone else

17

had despaired of finding them. They represent a concretely lived Hope. Yet, it may be thought that since this justice that the saints brought about was not institutionalized, it was incapable of producing a fundamental and overwhelming victory that would have transformed the economic, social, political, and cultural structures of a society.

Mauriac says this in a moving passage:

> "I was hungry and you gave me to eat; I was in prison and you came to me . . . as long as you did it for one of these, the least of my brethren, you did it for me." He was this prisoner; He was this hungry man. Through all hagiography, ever since there were saints to imitate the Lord, runs the legend of the poor man who knocks on a door in the evening, who is taken in or rejected, and who is Christ.
>
> But it is not really the legend that is important for us; it is history. Have men treated each other less cruelly from the day they began to believe in the Incarnate Word? In a recent sermon a well-known Jesuit poked fun at unsophisticated people like me who learn history from the poets. But (with all due respect to the good Father) I also learn history from the memoirs and letters of men who massacre and burn other men alive and who have committed such crimes while professing to believe that Christ too was a man.
>
> This is the question: has the Christian Era been marked by respect for man insofar as he has a suffering body capable of enduring much affliction, has a spirit that can be manipulated, has a conscience that can be broken down by torturing the body? Simone Weil was obsessed all her life by the millions of slaves who were crucified before Christ was born, by the immense forest of gibbets upon which so many precursors were nailed and to whom no centurion rendered homage after having heard their last cry. For my part, I am much more obsessed by all the crosses that have been constantly erected after Christ—erected by a blind and deaf Christianity which never recognizes in the poor bodies it submits to questioning the Christ whose pierced hands and feet Christians kiss so piously on Good Friday.

Why has this identity, which the Lord Himself established in terms which none can challenge, been grasped only by the saints or by those striving for sanctity? Certainly *they* are numerous; but why has this fact not been understood by Christian peoples? . . .

. . . There runs through Christian history, for all kinds of reasons, an attitude of invincible scorn toward less developed peoples. . . . The natural riches of underdeveloped countries has, without their willing it, released a covetousness among Christian nations: a vice which, in attempting to glut itself, has spilled much blood. Their domination is perpetuated by methods which testify that it is not the imitation of Jesus Christ but the imitation of His executioners that has too often been the rule of the Christian West in the course of history.

. . . But the course of history has not been influenced by the saints. They have acted upon hearts and souls; but history has remained criminal.[1]

It is the wish of the twentieth-century Church that the laity bring life to temporal structures in a Christian way. For this reason the birth-control problem is as much a community one as it is individual. World organizations concerned with planned parenthood meet in congress, as at New Delhi, to study this problem. It is important that Christians, preferably laymen, be present in order to make the Christian teaching known, since we believe it to be truer and more capable of integrating on the human plane a certain number of essential values. Through their participation in meetings such as these, which are seeking to bring about structural reforms, Christians can be effectual on a worldwide scale. In addition, the elements of a solution which they will bring with them and which spring from their Christianity will appear valid to others because they are true.

Catholics and Christians are making a very concerted effort today in this area. They are attempting to reach the structural level. I do not say that we must first change the structures before proclaiming the Gospel. Both must be done *together*.

Modern man is waiting for religion to be effectual on this point. M. Henri Spaak[2] once said: "Socialism has done more in sixty years to change concretely the living conditions of

thousands of men than two centuries of European civilization."
He said "European civilization" but was thinking "Christian
civilization." We must not hold Christian civilization responsible for this failure. Matters are more complex than that, but
it is good to take note of one modern reaction in the face of
this situation.

In his book *Ouragan sur le sucre*, which first appeared as a
series of articles in *France-Soir*, Sartre does not once speak of
religious problems. Nor will he ever encounter this problem. Up
to the present the Cubans had been led to believe that their
national economy was almost necessarily linked to sugar, the
island's sole produce. The United States bought the Cuban
stock at a price higher than the world market's. Because of this
Cuba was able to import automobiles, refrigerators, television
sets. Each time that a political change was on the verge of
becoming a reality, the country was threatened with no longer
having its sugar bought, or else with having to sell it at the
international price. For all practical purposes, then, only sugar
was being cultivated on the island. People worked only four
months out of twelve, for four months of work were enough.
On the other hand, on account of a lack of capital (which was
American) it was practically impossible to cultivate anything
else. A great section of extremely fertile Cuban territory near
Havana lay fallow. Castro risked seeing the American market
closed. The Soviet Union and other countries therefore pro-
posed to buy the sugar. Castro was able to introduce other types
of crops, like rice, which were perfectly feasible on the island.
He intended to start an industry that would refine the produce,
the raw materials, at home and thus create an internal market
that would raise the per capita income of the inhabitants.

To Sartre's mind, a man like Castro and those who worked
with him are bringing "salvation" to people who had been
living in little round thatched huts, teeming with children.
Castro brought social, economic and cultural justice. Man is a
being responsible for the universe which he must transform.
He must take stock of the human individual's place in a political
society. Here the political element interferes for the best and
for the worst. Man must transform the world politically and
therefore economically and sociologically. In a "religious" style,
Sartre describes the pre-Castro Cuban situation and the way in
which Castro began his revolution. He brings up the weeks

that followed this uprising. He tells of a day spent with Castro, almost in the style of court testimony. Christians have often heard of man in sin, man in unhappiness, threatened by death; but then came Christ, we are told. Sartre does not speak of sin, but he adds: then came Castro!

*   *   *

Once they have left religious faith behind, many atheists have the feeling that they have made a transition from the heaven of ideas to the earth of men.

In her book *Memoirs of a Dutiful Daughter*, Simone de Beauvoir mentions that she first lived an unreal religion that was individualistic and subjective. Here is her description of the piety of her young days:

> How comforting to know that He was there! I had been told that He cherished every single one of His creatures as if each were the one and only; His eye was upon me every instant, and all others were excluded from our divine conversations; I would forget them all, there would be only He and I in the world, and I felt I was a necessary part of His glory: my existence had an inestimable price. Nothing escaped Him: with even more finality than in my teachers' registers my acts, my thoughts, and my excellences were inscribed in Him for eternity; my faults and errors too, of course, but these were washed so clean in the waters of repentance that they shone just as brightly as my virtues. I never tired of admiring myself in that pure mirror that was without beginning or end. My reflection, all radiant with the joy I inspired in God's heart, consoled me for all my earthly shortcomings and failures; it saved me from the indifference, the injustice, and the misunderstandings of human nature. For God was always on my side; if I had done wrong in any way, at the very instant that I dropped upon my knees to ask His forgiveness He breathed upon my tarnished soul and restored to it all its luster; but usually, bathed as I was in His eternal radiance, the faults I was accused of simply melted away; in judg-

ing me, He justified me. He was the supreme arbiter who
found that I was always right. I loved Him with all the passion I brought to life itself.[3]

When she met Sartre, one might say that she "took her vows":

"He never stops thinking," Herbaud had told me. This
didn't mean that he cogitated over formulas and theories all
the time: he had a horror of pedantry. But his mind was
always alert. Torpor, somnolence, escapism, intellectual
dodges and truces, prudence, and respect were all unknown
to him. He was interested in everything and never took anything for granted. Confronted with an object, he would look
it straight on instead of trying to explain it away with a myth,
a word, an impression, or a preconceived idea: he wouldn't
let it go until he had grasped all its ins and outs and all its
multiple significations. He didn't ask himself what he ought
to think about it, or what would have been amusing or intelligent to think about it: he simply thought about it. . . .

We used to talk about all kinds of things, but especially
about a subject which interested me above all others: myself.
Whenever other people made attempts to analyze me, they
did so from the standpoint of their own little worlds, and this
used to exasperate me. But Sartre always tried to see me as
part of my own scheme of things, to understand me in the
light of my own set of values and attitudes. . . .

Apart from a few minor differences, I found a great resem-
blance between his attitude and my own. There was nothing
worldly in his ambitions. He reproved me for making use of
religious vocabulary, but he, too, was really seeking "salvation" in literature. . . .

. . . but they had all explored much more fundamentally
than I had the consequences of the inexistence of God and
brought their philosophy right down to earth.[4]

The notion of salvation as frequently presented seems unreal,
a kind of fatalism that is rather often expressed in terms of
the Gospel text: "The poor you will always have with you."

Father de Lubac's fine book *Proudhon et le catholicisme* sheds some light on this point. Proudhon called himself a theist and an anti-theist. He found himself faced with an inequitable economic, social, and political situation. He fought against the *right* of private property and for the *duty* of work. He wanted to "unfatalize" man's destiny and make him aware that he can and must change a situation which he has been told is impossible for him to change. At this time there was a kind of telescoping of Christian dogmas with a given socioeconomic situation, which in the period of the Second Empire passed for a divine order of things. This was the opinion of a certain number of Catholic theologians who never quite thought it through. As a reaction, in his attempt to "unfatalize" the situation, Proudhon did not have God for his target but rather the misalliance of the idea of God with a particular form of economic society.

If differing political ideas may be drawn from Holy Scripture, none has decisive and absolute value. From *Rerum Novarum* to *Pacem in Terris* the papal encyclicals connect their statements with a few essential points of revelation and with natural truths linked to revelation, but in them we also find *variables* that depend upon a particular point in time.

The theater of Bertolt Brecht is shown a great deal in Paris, Germany and the United States, and its aim is to lay bare real situations. For example, in *Mother Courage* the canteen-keeper has three children, two boys and a girl. Her business is keeping the canteen, and she needs the war to keep on living. At the same time she is against the war which will take away her sons and daughter. The name of this poor, torn woman is Mother Courage. Bertolt Brecht does not want us to commiserate with her out of compassion or pity, as did Aristotle in his tragedies and comedies. Brecht does not want the spectator to allow himself to be taken in by a tragic and fatal situation that would be impossible to change. In another one of Brecht's plays, *The Mother*, Pelagia Vlassovna, having lost her son who was executed at the time of the 1905 Revolution, tells the women who bring her a Bible and some soup that she is grateful for the soup because she is hungry but the Bible has no interest for her. People have told her about the many mansions in the heavenly Father's house, but there are too many people on earth, she feels, without a roof over their heads. When they tell her that her son died because it was God's will, even though

it might well be the case, she is not interested. All she knows is
that her son died on account of a very explainable decree of the
Tsar. At one point she is told by someone that if she had better
taught her son the Bible he would have been still alive. But
her answer is that even if he were alive, his life would hardly
be worth living. Then she turns upon her interlocutor and asks
why the only thing she fears is death. For the Mother, there
is no sense in fearing God. There are many people who tell
her, she says, that in God's house there are "many mansions,"
but no one who will explain why there is only too little dwelling space in Rostov.

Brecht wants to make the spectators aware that the woman's
unhappiness is very explainable and that action must be taken.
Marxist theater is opposed to religion as the "opiate of the
people." We can see this in *The Mother*. Brecht denies a salvation that would be a combination of fatalism and resignation.

It might be said that this is quite simplistic. Possibly, but
Brecht's plays are very frequently presented. The temptation
to identify certain situations with a pseudo-divine order crops up
again and again. For example, there are some surgical operations
that can turn an anxiety-ridden man into a person who looks at
the bright side of life, someone who is humorous and almost
clownlike (as sometimes happens in the case of a lobotomy).
Surely this operation may not be performed at whim, but the
moralists say that it can be done under certain circumstances.
We cannot be too quick to say that this is a sacred domain that
may not be touched. Quite often this "sacred" domain depends
on man. He is responsible for it and must transform it. When
Simone de Beauvoir asserts that there is no biological destiny of
woman from the viewpoint of motherhood, sexual psychology,
etc., it must not be said that she is wrong, or that she is giving
in to a Promethean temptation to pride. Perhaps there is some
truth in what she has to say about motherhood not defining
woman's destiny, not defining a woman's "being in the world."

Mistrust of the doctrine of salvation is also due to the fact
that it is often presented in a paternalistic form. In 1894 social
Catholicism was expounded in the light of medieval guilds, as we
see in *Rerum Novarum*. This formula may have been valid at the
time, but it is so no longer. Today, for example, the unions are
free and no longer under the protection of Church authority.

The problem is to know at what point "paternalistic" and

"maternalistic" vocabulary is no longer valid. The Church may judge that in some specific cases values that are essential to the life of grace are involved and require a particular stand, as for example in a question of a union dispute or political elections, the "opening toward the left," etc. In these instances we ought to obey the bishops even if we do not agree with them. Indeed, it is easy to say that in principle, but complicated to put it into practice. The rôle of Catholic publicists is to discuss these matters. In this area all necessary distinctions must be brought out. Too many texts still give the impression that there is a preestablished harmony between religious truths, on the one hand, and a rather totalitarian political power, on the other. The representation of those who speak in the people's name is looked upon here with a certain mistrust. As a result of Bossuet's *Discours sur l'histoire universelle* and his *Politique tirée de l'Ecriture Sainte*, we still have associations of images and ideas which tend in this direction. Leo XIII had said that all political regimes can be reconciled with the Church provided they respect the natural law. He was hardly listened to. We can therefore understand why so many men today have continued to be wary of churches in general and of the Roman Catholic Church in particular. For example, Camus stated that in the history of religions, and in that of the Church specifically, beliefs have become "ideologies," conceptual systems implying immediate applications on the societal plane. They have put their mark on a whole series of concrete institutions and have almost always ended up in totalitarian regimes, in a form of tyranny, and in those myths in whose name people are tortured and exiled. In this sense we can understand what he meant in *The Rebel* when he said that a real generosity towards the future consists in giving everything to the present.

The heritage of the wars of religion, the crusades, and the inquisition still weighs much more heavily than we might imagine on the opinion of the man of today regarding that notion of salvation that, to him, seems to be the notion of the Churches. For Camus, who undoubtedly saw it from the outside and from his own particular point of view, the Franco regime (which I shall not judge) seemed to be a social order where a series of human values were short-circuited by churchmen for the profit of a society that is declared to be Christian but is certainly not integrally Christian! Cardinal Pla y Deniel, the late primate of Spain, made this statement in regard to the concerns of the workers' unions in an extremely courageous letter published by the *Informations catholiques*. This shows quite well that the Spanish situation is much more complex than Camus was willing to believe when he told us, for example, in certain articles written in his youth, that Christ did not die for all those poor Spaniards. If Camus was oversimplifying, we too are oversimplifying. In the teaching of history we sometimes speak simplistically about the crusades. We rarely ask ourselves how the Eastern Christians look upon the crusades. We need merely read René Grousset's *La Croisade* in the collection *Que sais-je?* for the answer. In the crusades we see the glorious aspect of Christendom liberating the Holy Sepulcher, and are not concerned about how the Jews or Moslems may have reacted. Unconsciously, I am afraid, we have put into the heads of our children the idea of a triumphal Christendom, which is the exact opposite of our situation today, which has nothing triumphal about it.

I am not saying that all of the temporal and institutional elements of the Church that are still available to her ought to be suppressed. I am merely saying that we must be careful. Claudel's Catholicism has a whole series of biblical elements (which delights me) but there is also a baroque aspect to it. For me, the baroque era is prolongation of the triumphal Christendom of the Middle Ages into the modern world at the time of the religious wars. It is, so to speak, a "German Middle Ages." Along with evangelization and catechizing, people also made use of arms in their opposition to Protestantism, since it was unimaginable that a state could exist in which there was no political and religious unity.

Protestants reacted in the same way. At the time of the first break in the West, that of Lutheranism, fire was the answer. At the Diet of Augsburg in 1555, it was decided that Protestant countries were to remain Protestant and Catholic countries Catholic. *Cujus regio illius religio* was the cry. The ruler's religion was to be followed by his subjects. Catholics in a Protestant country had to leave their homeland. As was said at the time, they had the "benefit of emigration."

If France is poor in baroque monuments, the opposite is true in Belgium, Bavaria, Austria, and Spain. This baroque Catholicism was the expression of the triumph of Christ, his resurrection, but it also expressed a certain temporal triumph of "Christendom" that followed upon political victories which preserved Belgium, certain provinces of Austria, Bavaria, and the Rhineland for Catholicism.

Missionaries partially relied on the temporal power in their attempt at reevangelizing those regions that had been lost to Catholicism. This was the case in Bohemia after the battle of the White Mountain in 1622. The church of Santa Maria della Vittoria in Rome near the Termini station was built after this battle. The Emperor's troops and those of the Duke of Bavaria crushed the troops of the Calvinist Elector of the Palatinate and the Moravian troops that had wanted to defend certain freedoms from Bohemian Catholicism. Following this victory, Bohemia was "re-catholicized" in a manner about which I should prefer to say nothing. This is one of the keys of the religious drama going in today in Czechoslovakia. The building of a church after this victory attributed to the patronage of the Virgin can only be understood within the context of the age.

St. Peter's is also a baroque church. Bramante had wanted to erect the cupola of the Pantheon over the basilica of Constantine. He was to build a monument that would sum up all that was greatest in what ancient Rome had built: the dome of the Pantheon which still exists and the basilica of Constantine of which three arches remain. Michelangelo had the idea of transforming this cupola under the inspiration of Brunelleschi's in Florence. By its ascending movement, this cupola symbolizes a triumphant Christianity. St. Peter's then can be understood in two ways: the cupola that can be seen from every side represents a certain triumph of the counterreformation, of baroque Catholicism: but it was built over the tomb of Peter, who was martyred. The real Pantheon does not house heroes, in the ancient sense of word, but the fishermen of Galilee, the witnesses of the faith, the martyrs.

In speaking of salvation, we must distinguish between what has come from God our "Father" by means of the Church our "Mother"—the life of God, coming down from Heaven— and something accidentally inserted by a particular temporal regime. From this viewpoint, we must show modern man that the Church is *not* bound to authoritarian political forms.

II. LIFE AND LOVE

1. SURVIVAL

Modern man thinks of life, love, and death. Somewhere, Simone
de Beauvoir has told us that the clergy no longer speak to us
of death or of hell, giving the impression that perhaps they
no longer even believe in it. The best sermons on death are
made by atheistic writers like Camus, Sartre, Simone de Beauvoir, P. Warren, and Faulkner.

This would seem an excellent opportunity to recall the
essential truth of Christianity, the resurrection, for modern man
has an acute awareness of the frail and mortal character of the
human condition. But this is not, as we might have thought, a
stepping-stone for the proclamation of salvation, but rather a
reason to mistrust the good news of Christian salvation.

Here we meet with an extremely tangled psychological knot.
There is a great need for understanding, in the full sense of
the word. In one of his letters, Camus calls intellectual honesty,
which is most rare today, the hospitality of the mind. It
would be quite possible that there is some pride in this mistrust of Christian salvation: it is more courageous, more magnanimous to dedicate one's self to justice and the betterment
of the human condition with the knowledge that everything
ends with death; it is more magnanimous, more worthy of man
to be dedicated with this knowledge than in thinking that we
shall rise on the last day and that there will be a life continuing
after death. It is true that we have frequently an attitude here
that is more literary than lived, a kind of romanticism, a teen-
age twitch, a choice of revolt for revolution's sake. But we also
have the influence of Kant's categorical imperative, virtue for
virtue's sake, without reward. And we must further wonder why
this is such a generalized reaction. Here is what Simone de
Beauvoir writes on the subject after the passage where she tells
why she abandoned God:

> Yet the face of the universe changed. More than once dur-
> ing the days that followed, sitting under the copper beech
> or the silvery poplars I felt with anguish the emptiness of
> heaven. Until then, I had stood at the center of a living tab-
> leau whose colors and lighting God Himself had chosen; all

things murmured softly of His glory. Suddenly everything
fell silent. And what a silence! The earth was rolling through
space that was unseen by any eye, and lost on its immense
surface, I stood, alone, in the midst of sightless regions of the
air. Alone: for the first time I understood the terrible significance of the word. Alone: without a witness, without anyone
to speak to, without refuge. The breath in my body, the
blood in my veins, and all this hurly-burly in my head existed
for no one.[5]

A bit later, she adds:

I made another discovery. One afternoon, in Paris, I realized that I was condemned to death. I was alone in the house
and I did not attempt to control my despair: I screamed and
tore at the red carpet. And when, dazed, I got to my feet
again, I asked myself: "How do other people manage? How
shall *I* manage to. . . ." It seemed to me impossible that I
could live all through life with such horror gnawing at my
heart. When the reckoning comes, I thought, when you're
thirty or forty and you think "It'll be tomorrow," how on
earth can you bear the thought? Even more than death itself
I feared that terror which would soon be with me always.[6]

In the sequel, *The Prime of Life*, this obsession with death
reappears periodically and puts the finishing touches on this
book of over six hundred pages. At certain moments, Simone
de Beauvoir attempted a realization of her own death. She
tells us that no one is ever anything but a dead man with a
reprieve, in a state where we should prefer never to wake up.
When she was at the deathbed of her father, whom she greatly
admired, she tells us that her unbelieving father's decease was
a departure for nowhere; she was watching a peaceful return
to nothingness. This same theme can be seen again in her
novel *The Mandarins*, in *The Force of Circumstance* and in
A Very Easy Death.

Yet instead of this obsession with death, this "marginal
situation," bringing her to a reconsideration of the religious
problem and to a re-posing of the question as to whether the

proclamation of the resurrection and afterlife might not be the answer to the problem, her haunting memory is rather the reason for her mistrust.

In the works of Camus, the death theme began as a kind of décor, an underpainting that gave more pungency to the "honeymoon" going on openly between man and the world. In his later work, this theme becomes invasive, something like the situation in the cinema where a character who is lost in the crowd comes suddenly into focus. An example of this is found in "The Adulterous Woman" (1954). Janine, who has been married to Marcel for twenty-five years, travels alone with her husband on his trips through Algeria for his textile business. When she was a girl Marcel had often brought her to the beach. But since their marriage this had no longer been the case, partially from laziness and partially because he had to work and wanted to leave something for his wife in case of his death. He told her this over and over. Late one afternoon Janine found herself on a porch that looked out on the desert. She saw palm trees and the wide expanse of the desert, which was empty since it was growing cold. She thought about growing old. Already she was heavier and wearier. Surely she was still desirable, and she recalled the look on the faces of certain men on the bus. But then she thought of the girl she had been, pliant and supple, which she no longer was. That evening in her small hotel room, damp and wretched, she rejoins her husband:

> Then she dragged herself toward her bed, where Marcel came to join her and put the light out at once without asking anything of her. . . . She could feel only Marcel's warmth. For more than twenty years every night thus, in his warmth, just the two of them, even when ill, even when traveling, as at present. . . . Besides, what would she have done alone at home? No child! Wasn't that what she lacked? She didn't know. She simply followed Marcel, pleased to know that someone needed her. The only joy he gave her was the knowledge that she was necessary. . . . They made love in the dark by feel, without seeing each other. Is there another love than that of darkness, a love that would cry aloud in daylight? She didn't know, but she did know that Marcel needed her and

that she needed that need, that she lived on it night and day, at night especially—every night, when he didn't want to be alone, or to age or die, with that set expression he assumed which she occasionally recognized on other men's faces, the only common expression of those madmen hiding under an appearance of wisdom until the madness seizes them and hurls them desperately toward a woman's body to bury in it, without desire, everything terrifying that solitude and night reveals to them.[7]

This is man's true face beneath the mask of reason. A bit later Marcel falls asleep:

She cuddled a little closer and put her hand on his chest. And to herself she called him with the little love-name she had once given him, which they still used from time to time without even thinking of what they were saying.

She called him with all her heart. After all, she too needed him, his strength, his little eccentricities, and she too was afraid of death. "If I could overcome that fear, I'd be happy. . . ." Immediately, a nameless anguish seized her. She drew back from Marcel. No, she was overcoming nothing, she was not happy.[8]

Camus was haunted by the problem of death. At fifteen or sixteen, while walking along the beach in Algiers with Max-Pol Fouchet, he saw a small Arab run over by a bus. People ran to the scene and a crowd gathered. There was the father who said nothing, the mother wailing and the rubber-necked onlookers. Camus looked at the scene, moved somewhat further on, and then pointed at the sky and the crowd, saying to his friend: "See, Heaven doesn't answer." This episode was the inspiration for the narrative of the death of the son of Othon the judge in *The Plague*. Camus also said that the most absurd death was in an automobile accident. And this was how he himself died.

The situation we have just mentioned is called an "existential" situation in the vocabulary of modern philosophy.[9] How is it then that these exponents of modern sensibility, who have such an acute awareness of this "existential," are suspicious of the message of salvation?

1) Many confuse the doctrine of afterlife with the will for *individual* survival. They refuse to accept the projection into the other world of the physiological desire for survival experienced by every living being. The famous phrase "I have but one soul that I must save" seems to speak only of individual afterlife. Modern man says that he accepts death as long as his consciousness continues to exist in mankind. This was the opinion of Léon Brunschvicg. Roger Martin du Gard shows how Jean Barois, who was brought up as a Catholic in his childhood, lost the faith and became a militant secularist at the time of the Dreyfus affair. To his attitude the author opposes the attitude of Luce, one of Jean Barois's friends, who had also dedicated his life to the progress of mankind. Luce has children and is happy. He is well aware that he will have to give all that up. For him, there is nothing after death. Yet, he dies with a kind of hope for others which is just as total as his lack of hope for his own survival.

Woldsmuth, a friend of Jean Barois, describes Luce's death to him in this way:

> Not a single day did I ever see him waver in his acceptance of life and death; and yet he suffered terribly. He was engaged in reviewing his past life, as a whole. One morning, after a sleepless night, he said to me, "It's a consolation to me to see how harmonious my existence will have proved to be. While one's involved in active life, the feeling of a lack of unity of purpose often makes one feel despondent. But now I see I've little to complain of on that score. I've come across so many unhappy people, people who are always being flung this side or that from their true centre of gravity, and this makes them restless, dissatisfied. My life had none of these commotions; it could be summed up in two or three quite simple axioms. And this enables me to 'depart in peace.'
>
> "I was born with confidence in myself, in the daily tasks I shouldered, and in the future of mankind. The well-balanced life came easy to me. My lot was that of an apple tree planted in good soil that bears its fruit season after season."

The last week was particularly hard for him. But the day before he died he was in much less pain. His older grand-children came to the bedroom for a few moments. But by now he had almost ceased speaking. When he saw them entering, he said, "Go away, my dears, good-bye. I don't want you to see—that."

Towards six the lamps were lit. He looked round the room, as if to make sure all his children were present. There was something extraordinary in his gaze, as though at last he could see to the heart of things, nothing was hidden from him now. It seemed that, had he still been able to speak, he could have spoken the final, liberating word about himself, his life, the lives of all men. But propping himself on a shoulder he merely said, in a far-away voice, as though awak-ing from a dream, "Ah, this time it's death."

His daughters, kneeling round the bed, could not restrain their tears. Then he placed his hand on their heads, one by one, and murmured as if talking to himself, "How fine they are, my children!" Then sank back upon the pillow.

Night had fallen. Next morning he died, without having opened his eyes.

This is what I have been meaning for many days to write to you, my dear Barois; for I know the manner of our friend's dying will do you good, as it did to me. It consoles us for the disappointments we have encountered on our path. After seeing Luce die, I am more convinced than ever that I have not been wrong in staking my faith on human reason.[10]

On the contrary, Christian conversion and the hope for after-life as we have it in *Jean Barois* are caricatures. It leads one to think about what an Eskimo said to a missionary who was asking him about his religious belief: "We don't believe, Father, we are afraid!"

Since early morning Jean has been delirious. It is now eight in the evening. He awakes, feeling desperately tired. The room is full of shadows, and the movements of the living persons near his bed seem a continuation of his nightmare.

Suddenly he sees Cécile holding up a lamp. Abbé Lévys stands beside her, his clerical stole around his neck, and the vessel containing the holy oils in his hand.

A gust of panic sweeps him, his gaze shifts from one face to the other.

JEAN: "Am I going to die? Answer me, please. Am I dying?"

He does not hear their answer; a violent spasm of coughing tears at his lungs, half stifling him.

When he sees Cécile bending over the bed he clutches her to him in a desperate embrace. Gently she presses him back onto the pillows. He is too exhausted to resist, his eyes are shut, his breath comes in hissing gasps. The sheets are drenched in sweat.

Through the fever buzzing in his ears he hears the Latin phrases, while a cool film of oil is laid on his eyelids, ears, and palms.

JEAN: "Help, oh help me! Don't let me suffer!" His hands beat the air and, meeting the priest's long sleeves, cling to them as to the arms of a divine judge. "Are you sure He has forgiven me? Or . . ." In a last desperate effort he draws himself up from the pillow. ". . . hell fire?"

His mouth gapes on a cry of horror, then a moist râle rasps his throat. The Abbé holds the crucifix out to him; in a blind revolt he thrusts it away. Then his eyes fall on the effigy of Christ and, grasping the crucifix, he sinks back upon the pillow and crushes it passionately to his lips.

Too heavy for his feeble grasp, the crucifix slips from his hands. His limbs have ceased to respond to his will and seem to be receding from him. His heart-beats are a weak flutter, but thoughts race through his mind in wild confusion. Suddenly every fibre of his being grows tense; arrows of fiery pain flash across his body, through every vital cell. He makes some last convulsive movements. Then, immobility.[11]

This is the "closed religion" that Bergson described. In the face of death, this hole, this nothingness, seen above all as a threat hanging over individual life, the spontaneous and *instinctive* reaction is to want to disguise it, to cover it over. This is what Bergson calls the "fairy-tale function." It invents "fables" aimed at making us believe that death is not death. But what creates the problem is the survival of others, those we have *loved*. Then there is no question of a selfish will to live. If we look at the matter from this viewpoint, we shall have better luck with our dialogue with modern men, as Gabriel Marcel saw so well.

2) Therefore, *we must not confuse the problem of afterlife with the problem of the immortality of the soul.* An unbelieving woman novelist told me: "I would like to believe in afterlife. That would suit me very well, but to me it seems utterly impossible." Admittedly, there are philosophical proofs for the immortality of the soul, but there is a division between a proof that convinces theoretically as a necessary result of the sequence of reason and a concrete proof that frees us from the anguish of death. We must not forget that the Christian message here is not the immortality of the soul but the proclamation of the resurrection. We believe in it because we have faith in Jesus Christ. We know that God can do what is impossible for man.

Unamuno saw this basic problem. He had at one time been a socialist and said that socialism was capable of making men happier as a result of economic progress. But if they were not given at the same time a hope for immortality, a hope for survival for the "flesh and blood" man, all they would be receiving would be "the infelicity of bliss." Their happiness on earth would become still more risky because, since they had to leave this life, they would be leaving a better life than what they had previously known.

2. LOVE AND INTERSUBJECTIVITY

Unamuno posed the problem in terms of happiness or unhappiness. But it is not in these terms that the question ought to be posed. In *A la trace de Dieu*, Jacques Rivière was concerned with tracking God's "footsteps," which theology dubs "the fruits of grace," since grace as such is unknowable. The first thing to be done in order to take hold of the "fine dust" of the transcendent elements of events—and it is there to be found even though it is so easily swept away—is to place ourselves outside the context of interior satisfaction. We must begin by leaving aside our own personal happiness. From the beginning of its existence mankind has struggled for more happiness to exist, more charity, more understanding, more intelligence. What is the ultimate meaning behind this immense effort to live which is basically man's most profound *movement* —and it is impossible to put a stop to it in human history—if everything becomes nothingness at the moment of death? In this case the problem changes face, since we are no longer on the level of individual happiness but in the context of the *meaning* of man's history.

Modern thought stresses that man cannot abstract from his fellows, both on the level of solidarity and that of friendship and love. We have somehow rediscovered the sense of Arthur Rimbaud's remark: "The 'I' is an *other*." In describing a human situation, we cannot forget the importance of *intersubjectivity*. As an "existential" fact it has an ambiguous value. It always implies struggle. Hegel emphasizes that among human beings we have the dialectic of "the slave and the master." Human action ought to take up this struggle in a perspective of collaboration, solidarity, friendship, and ultimately love. We have therefore to run round that "circle" through which the spirit necessarily gets out of itself. The spirit cannot exist without a being that is presented *exteriorly* and as a threat. It must have a dialogue with this entity. Once it has taken up this battle and gradually succeeded in achieving solidarity, friendship, or love with it, the mind can return to itself.

In Camus's story, the love between Janine and Marcel is both a bond and a separation. Sartre's thought about Hell being "others" is especially in *No Exit*, a paradoxical way of saying something that is always true. The fact that the others are not only a Hell, but also *Hell* for us, a threat, a reality without which we cannot live, at any moment of our existence, a reality that both limits our freedom and must be accepted, is an obvious fact, an "existential." In intersubjectivity, there is struggle, loneliness, and setback.

Marguerite Duras' film-novel *Hiroshima mon amour* is representative from this point of view. In the film love is the only happiness possible for human beings. The happiness experienced by the girl with her German friend was romantic. It was lived as a totality, but this was abruptly brought to an end by the German's death when the city of Nevers was liberated. Later, married and with children, she met a Japanese. He too was married. He too had known the war at Hiroshima. Her meeting with him awakened in her the memory of the love that she had shared with the German. At the same time, she is aware that all of that is dead. In human love, to the extent that it was a particularly full experience, there is something that comes to destroy it: the war brought with it an awareness of a certain risk present in every human love.

In *Hiroshima mon amour*, the French girl loves the Japanese only through her memory of her love for the German. In the bar scene where she recounts the long story of her adolescent love-experiences at Nevers, the Japanese is a sort of catalyst, an occasion for remembering. Since her Nevers experience is also dead, her reminiscence is not liberating. There is no possibility of having a fresh look at the future, but only an evocation of those who have died, a chilling and fascinating presence of a dead love. The French girl is no longer at Nevers, not even in Hiroshima. She is nowhere. She no longer loves the Japanese or the German. She is turned to the past, fixed upon it, withered by her paralyzing memory. When the man to whom she is speaking adresses her in the familiar form of the second person singular he becomes both the Japanese and the German. Her love, then, is not a "communion," but rather a mutual fascination, in and with the death of everything and the blotting out of memories. Here is an example of the way she speaks to the Japanese:

HE: Do you scream?

(*The room at Nevers.*)

SHE: Not in the beginning; no, I don't scream: I call you softly.

HE: But I'm dead.

SHE: Nevertheless I call you. Even though you're dead. Then one day, I scream, I scream as loud as I can, like a deaf person would. That's when they put me in the cellar. To punish me.

HE: What do you scream?

SHE: Your German name. Only your name. I only have one memory left, your name.

(*Room at Nevers, mute screams.*)

SHE: I promise not to scream any more. Then they take me back to my room.

(*Room at Nevers. Lying down, one leg raised, filled with desire.*)

SHE: I want you so badly I can't bear it any more.

HE: Are you afraid?

SHE: I'm afraid. Everywhere. In the cellar. In my room.

HE: Of what?

(*Spots on the ceiling of the room at Nevers, terrifying objects at Nevers.*)

SHE: Of not ever seeing you again. Ever, ever.

(*They move closer together again, as at the beginning of the scene.*)[12]

At the night's end the French girl understands that she will again forget this "dead" love that she had forgotten. Everything will be oblivion, for memory itself is oblivion:

We're going to remain alone, my love.

The night will never end.

The sun will never rise again on anyone.

Never. Never more. At last.

You destroy me.

You're so good for me.

In good conscience, with good will, we'll mourn the departed day.

We'll have nothing else to do, nothing but to mourn the departed day.

And a time is going to come.

A time will come. When we'll no more know what thing it is that binds us. By slow degrees the word will fade from our memory.

Then it will disappear altogether.

Sartre presents the world of others as a threat that we can never disregard. Thus his picture of commuters waiting for the bus at Saint-Germain-des-Prés in the morning, queued up in the numerical order indicated by their ticket.

> There is a group of people on the Place Saint-Germain; they are waiting for a bus at the stop in front of the church. I am taking the word "group" here in the neutral sense: it is a gathering about which I do not yet know whether, as a group, it is the inert result of separate activities or a common reality that as such commands each one's acts, or a conventional or contractual organization. These persons, who are of very different sexes, classes and milieus, realize, within everyday banality, the relationship of loneliness, of reciprocity and of unification from without (and of massification from without) which characterizes, for example, the inhabitants of a large city insofar as they find themselves together, without being integrated by work, struggle or any other activity of an organized group which would be common to them. We must first of all point out that we are dealing here with a plurality of lonelinesses: these persons are not concerned with one another, they do not speak to one another, and in general do not even notice one another; they exist side by side around a traffic pole. . . . The bus reunites them as being their concern as individuals who *this morning* have business on the right bank, but already, as the 7:49 bus, it is *their interest as commuters*; everything is temporalized. . . . Yet, to the extent that the bus designates the commuters present, it constitutes them in their interchangeability: each is a product of the social whole, since he is united with his neighbors insofar as he is strictly identical to them . . . Each is the same as the Others insofar as he is Other than self.[14]

The passengers have become identified with their particular number on the line and are dependent on the number of seats available in the arriving bus. The individual is the captive of the series of commuters who came before him. We can never overlook these facts. We can never imagine that there is a little observatory outside of time from which height we would be able to disregard the situation. In the same vein, Sartre gives a description of himself in his office overlooking the Boulevard Saint-Germain. He is writing a book. He goes to the window, sees the red and green lights, the jammed up traffic and the drivers. He sees this as a series of obstacles and threats waiting for him once he leaves his office, finds himself on the sidewalk, having to cross the street.

> The field exists: actually, it surrounds us and conditions us; I have only to glance out the window: I will see men who are cars and whose drivers are cars, a policeman directing traffic at the street corner and, further on, an automatic signal directing traffic by its red and green lights, *a hundred exigencies* that come up to me from the ground, traffic jams, obligatory signs, prohibitions; collectives (a branch of the Crédit Lyonnais, a café, the church, apartment buildings, and also a visible seriality: people are in line in front of a shop), instruments (proclaiming with their congealed voices the way they are to be used, sidewalks, pavements, hackstands, bus stops, etc.). All these beings—neither things nor men, but the practical unity of man and the inert thing—all these summonses, all these exigencies do not yet concern me directly. In a moment I shall go down to the street and I shall be *their thing*, I shall buy this collective, a newspaper and the practico-inert totality that besets me and designates me will suddenly be laid bare through the total field as the Elsewhere of all Elsewheres (or the series of all the series of series). It is true that this reality, even though it is crushing or ensnaring, depending upon the case—and which teaches me, starting with elsewhere, my destiny as a petit-bourgeois Frenchman—is still an abstraction.[15]

Sartre calls this the *practico-inert*. The civilization that men have created is turned against them, and flies back on them like a boomerang. Sartre attempts to integrate the struggle-fear-opposition dimension into solidarity, for the benefit of a reality he calls the *group*. He gives us its genesis as a kind of "secular Pentecost." The revolutionary oath of a Communist cell is a sort of "baptism":

> In a sworn group, the basic relationship of all the members is that they were produced together out of the clay of necessity. . . . There is a kind of eternity of presence in the future. . . . It is the beginning of humanity. . . . We are the same because we have come out of the clay at the same date, one by the other through all the others. . . . We are brothers insofar as after the created act of the oath we are our own sons, our common invention. . . . Then man *is* sovereign.[16]

Then, in some way, mankind becomes its own child. It generates itself, and creates itself out of necessity. This vocabulary: new creature, baptism, sacrifice, slime of necessity, new mankind, mankind as its own son, is a sort of inverted use of Christian vocabulary. In the dialectic Communism wants to integrate violence and terror as an inevitable part of human history, it goes back to make it serve a purpose which it declares to be more human. Thus it goes back to Hegel.

*   *   *

Let us go further. In *The Condemned of Altona*, Franz von Gerlach feels responsible for the evil he did during the war against Russia. In his sister-in-law Johanna, who comes to visit him in the room where he has shut himself up, he sees a judge who is at the same time a friend, someone who judges him without condemning him. In this "love-trial" there is never any question of a life that could be genuinely communicated. Franz searches Johanna for a look that judges him, that knows the wrong he did but which at the same time forgives. He says to her: "Do you think that when you know all I have done you will still be able to look at me, still love me?" She answers: "I think so."

> FRANZ: . . . If a life is not sanctioned, the earth consumes it. That was the Old Testament. Here is the New. You shall be the future and the present; the world and myself. Beyond you there is nothing. You will make me forget the centuries. I shall live. You will listen to me, and I shall surprise your

looks; I shall hear you reply to me. One day perhaps, in years to come, you will recognize my innocence, and I shall know it. What a day of joyous celebration! You will be all to me, and all will acquit me. (*Pause.*) Johanna, is it possible? (*Pause.*)

JOHANNA: Yes.

FRANZ: Is it still possible to love me?

JOHANNA (*with a sad smile, but deeply sincere*): Unfortunately, yes.

(FRANZ *stands up. He appears relieved, almost happy. He goes to* JOHANNA *and takes her in his arms.*)

FRANZ: I shall never be alone again. . . .

JOHANNA: I'm not your judge. One doesn't judge those whom one loves.

FRANZ: And suppose you stop loving me? Won't that be a judgment? The final judgment?

JOHANNA: How could I?

FRANZ: By learning who I am.

JOHANNA: I already know.

FRANZ (*rubbing his hands with a cheerful air*): Oh, no. Not at all! Not at all! (*Pause. He looks quite mad.*) A day will come, just like any other day. I shall talk about myself, and you will listen. Then, suddenly, love will be shattered. You will look at me with horror, and I shall again become (*going down on his hands and knees and walking sideways*) . . . a crab.

JOHANNA (*looking at him in horror*): Stop!

FRANZ (*on his hands and knees*): You will look at me with those eyes, exactly like that. (*He stands up quickly.*) Condemned, eh? Condemned without right of appeal.[17]

For Sartre the love between the man and the woman is a confrontation parallel to the human condition, mortality and guilt, rather than an exchange. Separation, common confrontation are just as present as coalescence and communion. In *The Second Sex*, Simone de Beauvoir says that sexuality also manifests the extent to which two people are both alike and different. The more each one asserts his difference the closer they become, but at the same time they remain "others." Sexuality, she claims, never appears to us as defining a destiny but as the expression of the totality of a situation it contributes to defining. There is always a materialization of tension, heartbreak, joy, failure, and the triumph of existence in it. Actually, she maintains that physical love cannot be seen either as an absolute end nor as a mere means. It cannot justify an existence, but there is no alien justification for love either. What she is saying, then, is that love ought to play an episodic and autonomous role in every human life: above all it ought to be free.

She also specifies the tension that exists between difference and similitude. Continuing with her theme of physical love, she asserts that its fulfillment supposes that the woman succeeds in establishing a relationship of reciprocity with her partner. For her, the asymmetry of the male and female approaches to physical love creates insoluble problems as long as the "battle of the sexes" exists. These problems can be easily resolved if the woman senses both desire and respect in the man. But what she finds particularly upsetting is that two beings who together passionately deny and affirm their own limits, are both alike and different. Their difference too often isolates them, and yet when they come together it becomes a source of wonderment for them.

Finally, she lays great stress on the ambiguity of this experience. What she affirms as necessary for harmony is not refinements of technique, but rather a reciprocal generosity of body and soul which she bases on an immediate erotic attraction. This experience, she feels, is one that most poignantly shows human beings the ambiguity of their condition, since it involves both their bodies and their minds and makes them both "the other" and a subject.

We ought not have any illusions about sexual harmony as an absolute necessity without which married life would be a failure. Serious literature on the subject stresses the "being with" aspect, the communion, but also the fact that there is a frontier that cannot be crossed. We have here two psychological outlooks that cannot be completely fused, nor can either ever be *reduced* to the other. This is a law of love itself. People become one to the extent that there is acceptance of the other's being "other," that there can never be complete identification with the other's universe. The true human personality makes its appearance once we accept that the others exist, that they are the center of the world and we are not, and that we can never enter totally into their psychological makeup. Consequently, in some way we must accept the fact that in this encounter of solidarity, friendship, and love—and also from the sexual point of view—there will be tension, explosion, and inevitable rupture. Right within men's mutual encounter a new existential fact appears: there is nothing to bridge it. All functional deviations of the personality, of love—either on the sexual plane or on others—are connected, according to psychologists, with a form of narcissim. There is a desire to pursue one's own self, to observe one's self. In passing, this is the basic reason why all homosexual love affairs are unnatural. People look at themselves in a mirror. They see that they are so alike that there is nowhere else to go, no advancement to be made. In *Jean-Paul*, Marcel Guersant demonstrated this point in depth.

Loneliness, then, has to be accepted in our experience of "being with," not as something accidental, but as an essential element.

*   *   *

This way of looking at things could be a stepping-stone toward a Christian response. Here again, in Simone de Beauvoir, Marguerite Duras, and Paul Valéry, we come up against this same unreceptiveness. Our contemporaries are suspicious of salvation for they see in it a kind of stopgap. Their impression is that believers have ready-made answers, as if one could press a button on an automatic machine for the answer to the problem of death or the problem of love. They think that faith suppresses the flavor of life, its risks and its authenticity.

But the doctrine of Christian salvation does not imply this. In human love there is a point within the union beyond which we cannot go. The buckle cannot be refastened. And this is a sign. God communicates himself in love. In him we can love and rediscover those whom we love on earth. Those who have died remain with us to help us and the saints pass their time in heaven doing good on earth. Yet God reveals himself as a *hidden* God. "No one has ever seen God," St. John tells us

(1:18), "the only Son, who is in the bosom of the Father, he has made him known" (or, as we might say today, he has translated him for us). We can never fill the abyss separating us from him. Our happiness, as St. Gregory of Nyssa tells us, will be in discovering that in the beatific vision we shall always be uprooted from ourselves and projected ahead. *Epectasis* is an exploration that will never end, into the abyss of the super-essential Godhead. God is the hidden God. The mystics tell us that the cloud of unknowing—I do not say the unknowable—is a basic dimension of every approach to God. Not as a result of a certain complacency in the breach, but by virtue of religion. On this point the Old Testament is not abrogated but rather fulfilled by the New Law. The knowledge of God wrenches us out of ourselves; in the concrete circumstances in which we now find ourselves, we can never stop and "set out for glory." In leading us on, God makes it impossible for us to say: "Here is the Kingdom." David thought that his was "the Kingdom," but then came Solomon, the division, and the captivity in Babylonia. God acts in such a way that he never allows us to be completely satisfied. He merely gives us a "down payment."

In human love as enlightened by Christianity there are the first fruits of communion, friendship, and solidarity which oblige us to go further—to God himself. Ultimately, only God can respond to our aspirations, precisely because he keeps us from ever coming to a halt. He causes us constantly to come out of ourselves, even in the beatific vision.

Modern man accepts separation in love, failure in friendship, competition in solidarity, struggle in intersubjectivity. He bristles before a religion that speaks of consolation. When we hear a priest say at the end of a youth group mass: "Now, my friends, we shall thank God for the great grace that he has given us to attend mass," we are tempted to say: "We are not at mass to receive something, but to give something to God along with the others." This way of presenting religion as a con-solation is ambiguous. Bernanos told us that truth first frees and *then* it consoles. Of course there are "consolations" in religion. The message of Thérèse of Lisieux was *not* the shower of thorn-less roses. At the time, the Lisieux Carmel thought certain passages ought to be scored and replaced by less "scandalous" texts. Since the research done by Father Combes, we have the authentic text, which was later published by the Lisieux Carmel in 1957. To the extent that they came closer to God, the saints experienced "the night of the senses and the spirit" spoken of by St. John of the Cross. In biblical terms, God can be reached only by crossing the desert. This night—which consequently must not be confused with the anguish of despair—is described in this way by St. Thérèse:

> But all of a sudden the mist surrounding me became thicker, crept into my soul and so enveloped it that I can no longer find in it the gentle image of my Fatherland. Everything is gone! When I wish to rest my heart, wearied by the surrounding darkness, by recalling that country of light to which I aspire, my torment is doubled. It seems that the darkness has borrowed the voice of sinners and is saying mockingly to me: "You dream of the light, of a country scented with the most pleasant perfumes. You dream of the *eternal* possession of the Creator of all these wonders. You think that one day you will escape the clouds that surround you! Come, come, rejoice in the death which will give you not what you hope but a still darker night, the night of nothingness."[18]

In Montherlant's *Port-Royal*, Sister Angélique experiences *anguish*. Montherlant quotes six passages from the account of her captivity with the Ursulines. They have been put into a modern context. According to Montherlant, Sister Angélique asks herself if God exists:

> SISTER ANGÉLIQUE: Doubt . . . about everything to do with religion and Providence; doubt about whether the world is really so ordered as to justify us in living as we live. . . . What have I done to be so utterly deserted? . . . Did I pray? I don't know. I was in another world; I still am. And perhaps I only prayed with my tears. . . . I have gone in at the Gates of Darkness, with a horror which you cannot know, and which must not be known by anybody.[19]

The text of Sister Angélique's confession, edited by the Abbé Cognet, speaks of a *mystical ordeal*. The closer the nun came to

God, the more profoundly her will clung to God's will, and on the surface the more tormented and distressed everything was, the more marked was the disquiet expressed in Psalm 22: "My God, my God, why hast thou forsaken me?"

> God awakens with a ray of his light. Before, I used to think that he had exalted us too much, by giving us a share in the persecution of truth and righteousness. Now, instead, I found myself in such a profound state of humiliation, and so in the grasp of fear, that I almost did not dare raise my eyes to him. I looked upon all my sufferings as far less than what he had the right to inflict upon me, if he had wanted to treat me in the light of justice. . . .
>
> Then God granted me the gift of abandonment to the lead of his grace, not wanting me any longer to be concerned about myself, and of offering all I had suffered and all that still remained for me to suffer as the persecution continued, so that he might deign to take it in order to put aright all that I still owed to persons whom I had not served or supported as much as charity warranted. . . . I reserved nothing for myself but the hope of his mercy, which I saw as alone capable of satisfying the other boundless debts which I still owed his justice and goodness, and after having done this, I found myself more bereft than ever, although more calm.[20]

In regard to this dark night, Mother Angélique's account specifies that the suffering was in the senses and not in the depth of her soul. She "rejoiced in the spirit about what pained her in the senses" to the point that she remarked one day that her spirit was not humiliated sufficiently since she was concerned only about the glory there was in suffering for the truth.[21]
She also wrote:

> I have learned what despair is, since I had a rather clear glimpse of how one arrives at such a state, even though by God's grace these thoughts appeared very far from my heart, and it was merely an extraneous temptation that remained without, never disturbing me inwardly.[22]

III. LAW

1. GUILT

It has been said that modern man no longer has a sense of sin. This assertion requires many distinctions. What has happened, rather, is a displacement of the axis of morality. We may regret it, but we must understand it as well. Modern man tends to consider individual sin as of little importance. In his short book *Le Cas Françoise Sagan*, George Hourdin explains it. Between a man who is an unfaithful husband but also a serious-minded politician, doing what he can to better the economic situation of his constituents, and another who is faithful to his wife but is unconcerned about these other problems, the preference goes to the former. In other words, there is a tendency to put Gandhi, Lenin, and Charles de Foucauld all on the same plane, since all three, with their absolutely different and contradictory theories, have contributed toward the transformation of the lot of millions of men. It is thought that men who have done this are of a higher morality, since it is based on the axis of collectivity.

At the time of the 1956 Hungarian uprising, there was a worldwide wave of indignation. Some people left for Budapest during the few days that the border was open, and some never returned. The uprising was crushed and Kádar replaced Nagy. There was an attempt to blame it on people in the pay of Americans, reactionary members of the bourgeoisie. A student told me: "Private morality is of very little importance beside this public lie. That is what real mortal sin is! When I am with a girl, want to make out, and she does too, what importance does it have?" Certainly, as Camus has said, we do not put our minds in suspension "for a time" in order to "justify" violence; we have to attack the problem from all angles, and therefore also on the individual, personal level. The student's judgment is quite characteristic, however, especially when he added: "There are more important problems than an occasional necking session. . . ." Françoise Sagan once said: "My heroes hardly ever worry about the condition of the world and live in a way that you call immoral. They live in a world that could explode at any moment. Nobody wonders how the pieces will get picked up and put back together. Don't be so surprised that my heroes are like that!"

On the other hand, modern man has a very live sense of responsibility, that extends even to *guilt* before society, solidarity, friendship, love. In other words, guilt before the intersubjectivity necessary for the progress of mankind.

Here we have both a positive and a negative element, for this guilt is never that of a sinner before God. In this sense the notion of sin is absent, but there is an experience of responsibility that goes as far as guilt.

The writer William Faulkner is pervaded with the anguish of the white man's sin. In *Requiem for a Nun*, when Temple Drake confesses his crime to the Governor, Faulkner gives as a scene that mingles the creation of the world and the "creation" of the United States, especially the Southern states after the Civil War. The reader passes from one extreme to the other in sentences that never end, punctuated merely by semicolons for some twenty-five pages. Faulkner shows by this that Temple's sin in having allowed his child to smother to death is one small unit among innumerable other sins that were done before. Like the sea, they come to beat against the Governor's mansion. For the author, the Governor's mansion is the political and ideological epitome of the whole life of the State. We are in a "mythology" of creation, sin, responsibility, and need for redemption. In order to express the feeling of responsibility and guilt, to manifest the presence in man of a force driving him to destroy himself and others, because in man there is the dizzy fear of nothingness, Faulkner uses Christian symbols. Malraux has also said that there exists in man an instinct that drives him to build, but also to destroy. This "unbelieving Christian" disclosed a metaphysical root for this instinct, something inextricably mixed up with the human condition, as Dostoyevsky has already said.

In a prolongation of *Requiem for a Nun*, Camus made the same discovery. At seventeen he had read Dostoyevsky and especially *The Possessed*. In the theater adaptation he made of this work (the real title was *The Demons*), he placed at the heart of the play, at the beginning of the second part, the confession of that mysterious and elusive person, Stavrogin. The key to this character is the crime he committed when he allowed a girl he had violated to hang herself, while he waited patiently for a little red spider to reach the heart of a geranium. He knew that then Matryosha would be dead. By putting this confession at the heart of his adaptation of *The Possessed*, Camus showed that the heart of Stavrogin's problem is that he is unable to free himself from the haunting obsession of his crime.

We find this same problematical issue treated again in *The Fall*, the most ambiguous, the most "Gidian" and according to Sartre, probably the best work of Camus (who, however, did not like people to speak to him about it). He began it twice and destroyed the manuscript of the first version. Originally the story was to have been part of a collection containing six other stories from *The Exile and the Kingdom*. It progressed so well that it became necessary to publish it separately. It is the story of a great trial lawyer, Jean-Baptiste Clamence, who thinks he is a respectable man and is treated as such. One day while crossing a bridge over the Seine in Paris, he hears laughter behind him and wonders why people are laughing at him. He hears the laughter again at night in his bedroom. He opens the window and sees no one. He soon discovers that the whole universe is making fun of him. Then he rediscovers a memory which he had hidden deep inside himself three years ago and had purposely forgotten. One night, while crossing the same bridge, after leaving a girlfriend who undoubtedly was already asleep, he met a young woman who was leaning on the edge of the parapet. For an instant he desired her fresh and moist neck. He stopped imperceptibly and then moved on. Fifty yards further on along the bank he heard the frightful noise of a body hitting the water and then a scream. He did not jump into the water to save this other being. The next day he did not even try to find out what had happened.

Look, the rain has stopped! Be kind enough to walk home with me. I am strangely tired, not from having talked so much but at the mere thought of what I still have to say. Oh, well, a few words will suffice to relate my essential discovery. What's the use of saying more, anyway? For the statue to stand bare, the fine speeches must take flight like pigeons. So here goes. That particular night in November, two or three years before the evening when I thought I heard laughter behind me, I was returning to the Left Bank and my home by way of the Pont Royal. It was an hour past midnight, a fine rain was falling, a drizzle rather, that scattered the few people on the streets. I had just left a mistress, who was surely already asleep. I was enjoying that walk, a little numbed, my body calmed and irrigated by a flow of blood gentle as the falling rain. On the bridge I passed behind a figure leaning over the railing and seeming to stare at the river. On closer view, I made out a slim young woman dressed in black. The back of her neck, cool and damp between her dark hair and coat collar, stirred me. But I went on after a moment's hesitation. At the end of the bridge I followed the quays toward Saint-Michel, where I lived. I had already gone some fifty yards when I heard the sound—which, despite the distance, seemed dreadfully loud in the midnight silence—of a body striking the water. I stopped short, but without turning around. Almost at once I heard a cry, repeated several times, which was going downstream; then it suddenly ceased. The silence that followed, as the night suddenly stood still, seemed interminable. I wanted to run and yet didn't stir. I was trembling, I believe from cold and shock. I told myself that I had to be quick and I felt an irresistible weakness steal over me. I have forgotten what I thought then. "Too late, too far . . ." or something of the sort. I was still listening as I stood motionless. Then, slowly under the rain, I went away. I informed no one.

But here we are; here's my house, my shelter! Tomorrow? Yes, if you wish. I'd like to take you to the island of Marken so you can see the Zuider Zee. Let's meet at eleven at *Mexico City*. What? That woman? Oh, I don't know. Really I don't know. The next day and the days following, I didn't read the papers.[23]

A parallel episode is recounted by Julian Green in *Strange River*. On his way home one night, Philippe is walking along the Seine by the Passy port in Paris, and sees a woman in the distance being molested by a drunkard. He guesses that she is about to cry out and leans over the barrier, as if trying to hear her better. She sees him and, as the man is holding her arm and insulting her, looks at him pleadingly. Finally she calls out to

him with a hoarse low voice. But he does not move. Throughout his whole being there is a hesitation that lasts no longer
than a heartbeat, but seems interminable to him. He thinks to
himself, that perhaps before this moment he has never really
known himself. His hands, which have been glued to the stone,
suddenly spring off and he goes away.

Finally we may recall the tragic anecdote told by Georges
Duhamel in "Salavin," part of *The Lyonnais Club*. Salavin
wanted to be a saint, but the only time he had the possibility
of doing something heroic, on the occasion of a fire in a motion-
picture theater, he ran madly for the door to save his own skin.
At the Lyonnais Club, where people are discussing the revolution that is to transform the world, Salavin asks if the revolution
can really change it profoundly. His companions want to know
why he is so bent on changing the world. He bows his head and
tells them very quietly and hesitantly that it is because he is a
coward. At this point the entire audience grows silent as if
someone had said something indecent. And Salavin, like a
judged man, falls back into his seat.

Clamence discovered that he had been a coward. Memory of
this prevents him from living. He leaves Paris like a new mis-
anthrope. But, as his name indicates, he is also a new John the
Baptist, in a new wilderness of stones and water, which the
author places in Amsterdam. The confession made to an unseen
interlocutor is intended to show also that society in general, and
particularly Parisian society, deserves the deluge that will engulf
it. However, as the end of this confession without repentance
shows, Clamence is in bad faith in wishing to dilute his personal
guilt in a general guilt. He asks his interlocutor to repeat what
what he has been saying for months to himself, telling the girl
to throw herself in the water again so that they both might have
another chance to save themselves.

Camus used the word "guilt" in a letter to one of my friends.
This guilt cannot be reduced to anything other than itself.
We must take it on ourselves. Here we find ourselves faced
with an act that it is impossible to assume: this is a "limit
situation." Clamence no longer believes. It is impossible for him
to go back, to make the wheel of time turn back. There is no
God to whom he can entrust the one whom he abandoned.
There is no God before whom and with whose help he can
atone in order to save others.

In Faulkner's play which Camus adapted, the black woman tells Temple Drake at the end of the third act that there must certainly be a place somewhere where children no longer remember us, not even these hands that smothered them. In other words, there is a place where the child whom we let die will have forgotten the crime we committed, for there is a hope of salvation.

What light can be brought by faith appears in Clamence's testimony in the course of this "confession" as judge-penitent:

> God's sole usefulness would be to guarantee innocence, and I am inclined to see religion rather as a huge laundering venture—as it was once but briefly, for exactly three years, and it wasn't called religion. Since then, soap has been lacking, our faces are dirty, and we wipe one another's noses. All dunces, all punished, let's all spit on one another and—hurry! to the little-ease! Each tries to spit first, that's all.[24]

The soap was lacking: it happens that another writer used this image in a similar context. A Jewish artist, pursued by Christ's call since the age of seventeen, finally allowed himself to be baptized by Father Gillet during the summer of 1926. He was thirty-one. In *Moi, Juif, livre posthume,* René Schwob shows that he did not yet believe in Jesus' divinity. He saw in him only the man described by the Gospels. He merely accepted baptism "without pleasure," without excluding (otherwise he could not have been baptized) the divinity of Jesus but without having an unshakable certainty about it. The *Journal* kept by René Schwob from the summer of 1926 to Easter, 1927, shows us how, upon recovering from an illness, almost daily communion and use of confession brought this pilgrim progressively to a total faith in Jesus the Son of God:

> I began with a confession. Since I had to cleanse myself of something I had done which—even though I felt it was not sinful—still weighed upon me, for its image was glued to me and bound me to a kind of revolting complicity. The miracle of confession is that it can be like soap and leave no trace. . . . Confession gives the soul a taste for austerity. . . . Without it, it is not possible to make a real recovery.

Austerity is physically absent. Confession does away with the problem. It does away with the "dirty oil," as Claudel assured me. . . . I know that confession is needful to purify the soul and allow it to come back to God—that without this recourse supernatural life is destroyed by sin—but also that this recourse is sufficient to be reborn to grace just as if sin could be absolutely dissolved. . . . So today, this new sin affects me more painfully, but without despair. . . . The kernel of Christ's teaching is that it gives us the strength to start all over again. . . . This is the time of the new flood and the new Noah's ark.[25]

2. Need for a Judge

In *The Condemned of Altona* of Sartre, the character Franz von Gerlach was pure. Péguy might have said that his hands were pure because he had no hands. He was deeply troubled by his father's complicity with the Nazi regime. During the Russian campaign Franz had tortured prisoners to make them talk. At the war's end, he shut himself up in a room of his family's house. His sister came to see him every day, and brought him his food. He would no longer see his father. People had made him believe that Germany was still at its worst, that in Düsseldorf there were innocent orphans who were dying: there had been a service in a roofless, deserted church for nine hundred little coffins. If Germany is still in this slough of despondency, eighteen years after the end of the war, everyone is guilty and no one is guilty. Franz too wants to dilute his personal guilt in a more general guilt.[26] When his sister-in-law Johanna comes on stage and he sees her as a well-dressed and attractive woman, he comes to the realization that Germany is not in its throes. And by this very fact he is obliged to face his guilt, and to assume it. As we have already seen, what Franz wants from Johanna is a judgment that is also an uncondemning love, which does not kill. He fails. Then a new dimension appears in the play, and probably the one Sartre had in mind from the beginning. Having failed with Johanna, Franz agrees to see his father. His father is going to die in six months. He has throat cancer and knows it. The father appears only in this context in the play. All the other characters have name and surname, but we never know what the father's name is. He is merely "the father." This is what he is called by his children in a way that is sardonic, loving, and admiring. Franz tells him that he (the father) will not judge him because he has no right to do so, since he holds his father responsible for the murder of a Polish rabbi whom he may have denounced. He concludes that for him his father is no longer a father:

FRANZ: . . . You won't be my judge.

FATHER: Who's talking of that?

FRANZ: It's in your eyes. (*Pause.*) Two criminals. One condemns the other in the name of principles they have both violated. What do you call that farce?

FATHER (*calmly and without expression*): Justice. (*A short pause.*) Are you a criminal?

FRANZ: Yes. So are you. (*Pause.*) I don't accept your competence to judge me.

FATHER: Then why did you want to speak to me?

FRANZ: To tell you I've lost everything, and you'll lose everything. (*Pause.*) Swear on the Bible that you will not judge me![27]

But later, he asks his father to judge him:

. . . I'm not sure about anything I've told you—except that I tortured them.

FATHER: And then what? (FRANZ *shrugs his shoulders.*) You kept on walking? You hid? Then you came home?

FRANZ: Yes. (*Pause.*) The ruins gave me my justification; I loved our looted houses and our mutilated children. I pretended that I was locking myself up so that I shouldn't witness Germany's agony. It's a lie. I wanted my country to die, and I shut myself up so that I shouldn't be a witness to its resurrection. (*Pause.*) Judge me!

FATHER: You made me swear on the Bible. . . .

FRANZ: I've changed my mind. Let's get it over with.

FATHER: No.

FRANZ: I tell you, I release you from your oath.

FATHER: Would the torturer accept the verdict of the informer?

FRANZ: There isn't a God, is there?

FATHER: I'm afraid there isn't. It's rather a nuisance at times.

FRANZ: Then, informer or no informer, you're my natural judge. (*Pause. The* FATHER *shakes his head.*)[28]

Implicit in this last interview between the father and son is the fact that man needs a law, he needs someone to tell him what is good and bad. Man looks for a law that will judge him, but one that at the same time gives life. Consequently, he is looking for a father, since on the phenomenological plane the idea of law-judgment and law-life is very profoundly bound up with the father image. This is why, when this reality of the law is transgressed by those who have a responsibility of the same kind in society, a wound is made in the soul from which it rarely recovers.

When Franz learns that his father had been aware for a long time of the criminal acts he had committed, he exclaims:

. . . For God's sake what did you think?

FATHER (*with deep tenderness*): My poor boy!

FRANZ: What?

FATHER: You ask me what I thought, and I'm telling you. (*Pause.* FRANZ *stands up straight, then he collapses, sobbing, on his* FATHER's *shoulder.*) My poor boy! (*He awkwardly caresses the back of* FRANZ's *neck.*) My poor boy![29]

Since this is not a play by Casimir Delavigne that we are reading, this moment of paternal-filial recognition, which is unique in Sartre's work, gives evidence of the necessity of the paternal bond.

A short time later, the father asks his son for forgiveness, and Franz becomes frozen with fear and shock. He asks his father why, and the answer comes back that the father wants to be pardoned for having given Franz a future which is nothing else but his own past.

At the very moment that the mediation of the father appears, it is destroyed and negated by its opposite: the future wished by the father for Franz was merely the father's past; the father had never really engendered his son. And so the son, frozen with fear, thinks he can make a deal. Rarely has anyone demonstrated so skillfully both the necessary presence and radical absence of a fatherly relationship.

The only thing left is death. The father tells Franz that since he made him he will also unmake him. His death will envelop Franz's, and he will be alone in dying.

It is as if the father wanted to make the birth of his son, his filiation, something that had never been. He wants to "re-engender" his own son, to give him a second chance in a kind of re-generation that would be a birth in reverse. We now can understand Franz's reaction. Life bursting beneath an empty sky is comical, meaningless. Franz finds himself in the shadow of a cloud, a storm, and the sun will shed light on the place where he lived. He does not care, since gain is loss.

The father "re-engenders" him *in death*. Father and son commit suicide in the family Porsche, going ninety miles an hour off the parapet of the Elbe bridge.

3. Need for a Father

Kafka's works shed light here. Differing from some of the characters of Sartre, Gide, Camus, or Malraux, Kafka was always persuaded that man needed a law and that this law was represented by the father. Certainly, for him, Kafka's father was a kind of bogey, an enigmatic idol of fatherhood, an abitrary authority. Kafka was a sick man. But instead of "liquidating" paternal values, he reversed the problem: there is a promised land, a law, a father; Kafka himself never reached this promised land; he was always condemned by his father, prevented from living on account of his father, paralyzed by him, but he never denied paternal authority. Guilt implies a law. It must be rediscovered in the flesh, in the concrete mediation of fatherhood. In Sartre's world, there is the absence but also the impossibility of encountering the father,[30] for to look for the Father-Judge is to escape one's personal responsibility. Sartre's characters want to "liquidate" paternal values. On the contrary with Kafka, instead of attacking the father's world by saying that he himself is right, he says that it is his father who is right and he who is wrong.

Kafka has said of himself that he was either an end or a beginning. And in his notebook he specified: "In the struggle between yourself and the world, second the world." His characters, Joseph K., the hero of *The Trial* and K., the land-surveyor in *The Castle* are not depicted as innocents, tossed into an "absurd" world, but as *guilty* men who cut off the essential link of their roots in the soil, the family, the law. Kafka's world is not that of the absurd, of "non-meaning," but of a state where the "promised land" which is the world is closed off to man. He has lost the sense of the law and wanders his whole life long before the "gate of the law." Kafka said of himself that he was a kind of "secular Moses." He is one of those who affirm the existence of a promised land even if they never reach it. Unlike many modern heroes in literature who accuse the world of being absurd, or at least an enigma, and look upon themselves as poor innocents, Kafka continues to stress the existence of a land of promise. He accuses himself, with humility. I know of few more pregnant lines, since they are so marked with the spirit of Israel, than these in which Kafka sums up these thoughts:

> It is not inertia, ill will, awkwardness—even if there is something of all this in it, because "vermin is born of the void"—that cause me to fail, or not even to get near failings: family life, friendship, marriage, profession, literature. It is not that, but the lack of ground underfoot, of air, of the commandment. It is my task to create these, not in order that I may then, as it were, catch up with what I have missed, but in order that I shall have missed nothing, for the task is as good as any other. It is indeed the most primal task of all, or at least the reflection of that task, just as one may, on climbing to heights where the air is thin, suddenly step into the light of the far-distant sun. And this is no exceptional task, either; it is sure to have been set often before. True, I don't know whether it has ever been set to such a degree. I have brought nothing with me of what life requires, so far as I know, but only the universal human weakness. With this—in this respect it is gigantic strength—I have vigorously absorbed the negative element of the age in which I live, an age that

is, of course, very close to me, which I have no right ever to fight against, but as it were a right to represent. The slight amount of the positive, and also of the extreme negative, which capsizes into the positive, are something in which I have had no hereditary share. I have not been guided into life by the hand of Christianity—admittedly now slack and failing—as Kierkegaard was, and have not caught the hem of the Jewish prayer shawl—now flying away from us—as the Zionists have. I am an end or a beginning.[31]

At times a light pierces this night, for example when Kafka asserts that we are living as if we were the sole masters, which ultimately makes us beggars.[32] It is apparent also in this text:

> Humility provides everyone, even him who despairs in solitude, with the strongest relationship to his fellow man, and this immediately, though, of course, only in the case of complete and permanent humility. It can do this because it is the true language of prayer, at once adoration and the firmest of unions. The relationship to one's fellow man is the relationship of striving; it is from prayer that one draws the strength for one's striving.[33]

This "promised land" is love: it is

> The infinite, deep, warm, saving happiness of sitting beside the cradle of one's child opposite its mother.
> There is in it also something of this feeling: matters no longer rest with you, unless you wish it so. In contrast, this feeling of those who have no children: it perpetually rests with you, whether you will or no, every moment to the end, every nerve-racking moment, it perpetually rests with you, and without result. Sisyphus was a bachelor.[34]

"We must think of Sisyphus as being happy," Camus wrote. Kafka tells us: "Sisyphus was a bachelor." Two worlds collide here and stand in opposition to each other. Kafka gives a hint as to the sense that the lack of law, father, and love reveals to anyone who knows how to read the signs. Depending upon whether one accuses the world or one's self, the same deeds, the same derelictions change their stamp.

It is not astonishing then when we see that Kafka, who despite all this refrained to the end from any religious statement whatsoever, could still have written this short apologue:

> One of the first signs of the beginnings of understanding is the wish to die. This life appears unbearable, another unattainable. One is no longer ashamed of wanting to die; one asks to be moved from the old cell, which one hates, to a new one, which one will only in time come to hate. In this there is also a residue of belief that during the move the master [*der Herr*] will chance to come along the corridor, look at the prisoner and say: "This man is not to be locked up again. He is to come to me [*er kommt zu Mir*]."[35]

NOTES TO CHAPTER 3

1. François Mauriac, *The Son of Man*, trans. Bernard Murchland (Cleveland and New York: World 1960), pp. 111–118.

2. Paul-Henri Spaak, former Socialist Prime Minister of Belgium.

3. Simone de Beauvoir, *Memoirs of a Dutiful Daughter*, trans. James Kirkup (Cleveland and New York: World, 1959), p. 78.

4. *Ibid.*, pp. 360, 361, 362, 365.

5. *Ibid.*, pp. 145–146.

6. *Ibid.*, p. 146.

7. Albert Camus, *The Fall and Exile and the Kingdom*, translated by Justin O'Brien (New York: Modern Library, 1956), pp. 174–177.

8. *Ibid.*, pp. 176–177.

9. Here a distinction is made between *existentiels* and *existentials*. *Existentials* are those situations that no man, no matter what latitude or age he has lived in, can ignore: death is one of these *existentials*. *Existentiels* designate concrete situations — we are French, Belgian, American, sick, intelligent, rich, poor, etc.—and these we can no less ignore, although they vary with the individual.

10. Roger Martin du Gard, *Jean Barois*, trans. Stuart Gilbert (New York: Viking, 1949), pp. 360–362.

11. *Ibid.*, pp. 362–363.

12. Marguerite Duras, *Hiroshima mon amour*, trans. Richard Seaver (New York: Grove, 1961), pp. 57–58.

13. *Ibid.*, p. 77.

14. Jean-Paul Sartre, *Critique de la raison dialectique*, I (Paris: © Editions Gallimard, 1960), pp. 308, 311. Italics and capitalization are the author's.

15. *Ibid.*, pp. 362–363.

16. *Ibid.*, pp. 451–453, 588.

17. Jean-Paul Sartre, *The Condemned of Altona*, trans. Sylvia and George Leeson (New York: Knopf, 1961), pp. 134–135.

18. St. Thérèse of Lisieux, *Manuscrits autobiographiques* (Edition Office central de Lisieux, 1957), p. 252.

19. Henri de Montherlant, *Port Royal* (New York: Hill and Wang, 1962), pp. 143–144.

20. Mère Angélique de Saint-Jean, "Relation de captivité," in *La Table ronde*, December, 1954, p. 50.

21. *Ibid.*, p. 47.

22. *Ibid.*, p. 50.

23. Camus, *The Fall and Exile and the Kingdom*, pp. 69–71.

24. *Ibid.*, p. 111.

25. René Schwob, *Moi, Juif* (Paris: Libraire Plon, 1928), pp. 230, 279–281, 342, 352.

26. I am certain for my part that Camus's *The Fall* was Sartre's inspiration for *The Condemned of Altona*.

27. Sartre, *The Condemned of Altona*, p. 160.

28. *Ibid.*, pp. 164–165.

29. *Ibid.*, p. 168.

30. In *The Words*, Sartre shows the absence of a father in his childhood (he was brought up by his grandfather); but he makes a transition from the absence of a father to the impossibility of ever finding him.

31. Franz Kafka, *Dearest Father*, trans. Ernst Kaiser and Eithne Wilkins (New York: Schocken, 1954), pp. 99–100. The text dates from 1918.

32. Cf. G. Janouch, *Conversations With Kafka* (New York: Praeger, 1953).

33. *Dearest Father*, p. 47.

34. *The Diaries of Franz Kafka 1914–1923*, ed. Max Brod (New York: Schocken, 1949), pp. 204–205.

35. *Dearest Father*, p. 35.

4

Salvation as Subjective

CHRISTIAN SALVATION IS A GIFT. TO RECEIVE THIS GIFT WE HAVE
to be receptive and available. God speaks to us in Scripture. He
speaks to us in the Church. We must listen to him and respond.
We have to believe in him. Faith is an act of obedience to a
grace received, and man's affirmation is one more gift from God.
Modern man, however, is suspicious of the attitude demanded
by salvation: to accept God's gift. This is how Sartre can identify availability and passivity.

I. RESPONSIBILITY AND VALUE

At the heart of the modern notion of man we find the concept
of responsibility. Man is a being that has to make himself, to
"create" himself on his own.

Up to the Renaissance, man was looked upon as a microcosm,
a part of the universe. He was the manifestation of the sacred
presence of God acting in nature. Cistercian piety, for example,
was characterized by a very profound sense of the sacred. The
Cistercian churches, sober and austere as they were, "sacralized"
their natural surroundings: the valley where the monastery was
built, its calm, and the quiet of the wood nearby. In nature,
which the monastery transfigured, the monk found a diffused
presence of God.

The modern age is under the sign of subjectivity, of the
autonomy of the mind, of responsibility as it is seen in idealism.
. . . Is not a religion of inwardness, of subjectivity, of the pres-

ence of God in our soul, a kind of sacralization of this modern
outlook?

Today, these two aspects are brought together: responsibility
and freedom are exercized in a concrete world of obstacles and
values. Actually, man is responsible for the universe. He transforms it economically, socially and politically, thanks to the
progress of science and technology. He gives it meaning. We
make the transition then from a cosmological vision to an
anthropological one.

Consequently, man is not discovering laws *inscribed* in nature
which merely have to be brought to light through instruments
that are increasingly perfected. These "laws" are a "creation"
of the human mind but without being arbitrary or subjective,
since the universe "responds" to these laws; we can act on it and
"direct" it.

In the mystery of the family as analyzed by Gabriel Marcel,
there is a reality of a special kind. If all the members renounced
the family its mystery would cease to be. Family values, then,
exist to the extent that each member makes them exist by
choice, by his adherence. They do not exist somewhere in
reserve. They depend upon us. Yet these same family values are
not purely subjective. When members of a family cling together,
they discover real values which are inherent in the family context and bound up with this type of encounter, with this
personal communion.

The esthetic experience has the same significance. The artist
creates and what he creates has universal value. In creating, he
discovers a lost country. He rediscovers himself. And the same is
true for all truly human experiences. At the core of all these
realities is the involvement of the free person. Once he has
become involved, he always finds his lost homeland, which he
discovers is nearby but inaccessible.

In *Rome n'est plus dans Rome*, Gabriel Marcel gives a
description of the absence of the family "mystery." Marc-André
has relatives who no longer know what the meaning of their
life is. He is therefore rootless. He incarnates a dispossessed
generation, as Pascal Laumière [Marc-André's uncle] says to
his wife:

> "You know, all during that conversation, I sensed very
> painfully that I was unable to help this boy, to strengthen
> him. What he told me in confidence. . . . It's awful. . . .

He is part of a generation that is the most dispossessed the world has ever known. He doesn't believe in anything any more."[1]

Marc-André gives a lucid description of what these life "values" could be, were they mediated by the mystery of the family:

"You have lived. I don't know too well what your life was all about, but you wrote, you did love, you believed in things . . . although I don't know what they were. But for you the word "future" has in no way the same meaning it has for us. You must feel that you accomplished at least some kind of vocation."[2]

Somewhat later, he says to his uncle:

"Have you said even one word that would make me change my ideas? If only you could have been absolutely sincere in saying to me that God's will was for me to stay, that by leaving I would be disobeying God."

"Would that have convinced you?"

"Maybe. If your words had something in them that could make me love this finicky God, if in a flash he had become our own God, yours and mine."[3]

On the other hand, the father of one of his friends raises this hope in him:

"The father of my friend Denis Moreuil, who is a true believer—maybe the only one I've met—is an engineer, and he just refused a job offered to him in Mexico. He told his son: 'You know, I have no idea what would happen to me. It might be a total failure. I don't overestimate myself at all. But I believe in God. I'm counting that he won't desert me, and that he will spare me the final disgrace. Either he will take me or else give me the strength to bear what he has in store.' These are words that find an echo in me, only, that kind of faith I find almost incomprehensible."[4]

Again, as we have seen, love between two people can exist only if they have chosen to love one another. When they have given a new meaning to their lives they do not have the impression of creating a world, but rather of discovering a lost country, of discovering themselves in an already existing country which they would never have discovered if they had not exchanged their pledge together.

II. SONSHIP

If the gift of grace is presented in a climate of fear and constraint, adherence to it will be an alienation and involvement in it will be warped. If fear of God is frequently mentioned in revelation, this "fear" has nothing in common with craven fear. St. Paul tells us we are not slaves but sons. It is this gift of sonship that furnishes us with the key to the mystery of grace.

God is a Father, the Father of all men. The notion of fatherhood is essential; but it can be quite misleading and it also must be properly understood.

What fatherhood basically is, is the creation of a living image that is not a reflection of one's own complacency with oneself but an image which on the contrary can enter into a dialogue with the father. The son has received everything from the father. He is totally dependent on him but he is also free. The son therefore becomes a co-citizen, an *Ebenbürtig* of his father. He enters into the father's world. What is essential in this father-son relationship is the polarity, the tension inside the world they form together.

In his letter to his father, Kafka explains the meaning of marriage:

> Precisely this close relation does indeed partly lure me towards marrying. I picture this equality that would then arise between us, and which you would be able to understand better than any other form of equality, as so beautiful precisely because I could then be a free, grateful, guiltless, upright son, and you could be an untroubled, untyrannical, sympathetic, contented father.[5]

The Bible reveals to us that man has been called by God to supernatural life. God takes the initiative in this call. He has created man in his image. There is not identity between God and man, but likeness. God has communicated to man all that he can communicate of himself. The incommunicable is communicated while still remaining incommunicable. Man becomes God's heir, the heir of all that he can receive. He is made king over creation.

The mystery of sonship finds all its truth in the mystery of the incarnation, in the birth of the new Adam, a "translation" in human language of God's life.

The new Adam gives us the true vision of man. By virtue of the hypostatic union, his human nature acts in perfect communion with his divine nature. As a result of this union, through the grace and unction of the Holy Spirit, his human nature is not mutilated or impoverished. It is even *because of his union with the Father* that Jesus is king of creation and that he achieves this total dominion over the world, of which the resurrection is the great sign. The root of Christ's kingship over the world—and consequently of our kingship—is constituted precisely by this "total passivity," or, more precisely, by this active receptivity, the acceptance of the omnipotence of God vivifying Jesus' humanity. It is the perfect image of the Father, an image that is manifested.

Being disposed and receptive has nothing in common with inertia or negative passivity. Jean-Paul Sartre has never thought of a gift as anything other than a threat, a pitfall. As a result possibly of his childhood, his first reaction to life is one of mistrust. On the other hand, for Gabriel Marcel, life is looked upon as an exile: his early childhood left him with the memory of a happiness lost. For him man's vocation, then, is an invitation to rediscover what has been lost. While Sartre never had the feeling of a "homeland," Marcel puts this at the center of his work, because it was at the center of his life.

I was almost four when I lost my mother. Independently from the rare precise images that I was able to keep of her, she remained present to me; mysteriously she has always been with me. However, my aunt, as gifted perhaps but very different, was inevitably to overshadow her in fact; and I think I understand today that strange duality at the center of my life between a deceased person, about whom we spoke quite rarely either because of our despair or out of modesty

—and a kind of reverential fear kept me from asking questions about her—and another person who was extraordinarily forceful and domineering, and who thought herself obliged to shed light on the smallest recesses of my existence. I suspect that this disparity or this secret polarity of the invisible and the visible exerted upon my thought, and far beyond my expressed thought, upon my very being, an occult influence that infinitely surpassed all those other influences with discernable traces in my writings.[6]

According to what he told F. Jeanson about himself, Sartre, on the contrary, feels like a "counterfeit mongrel," totally accepted and yet not at all justified. He lived with his mother at the home of his grandparents. Sartre confides in his friend: "My grandfather was very much of an actor, and so was I. All children are, more or less."

Since his grandfather's voice was dominating for him, because it was to a certain extent the father voice, or at least the voice of the only man in the family, the actor's tone of this voice was enough to denounce existence as absurd and the play as the means used by men to hide this absurdity from themselves:

I never knew the feeling of owning something. Nothing ever belonged to me, since at first I lived with my grandparents and after my mother's remarriage I was all the more unable to feel at home in my stepfather's house.[7]

We now can understand how Sartre could say about Jean Genêt, who as a youth was brought up in a reformatory as a result of having been caught in a theft: "Treated as a thief at seventeen, Genêt would have taken it as a joke; that is the age when we liquidate paternal values."[8] The same feeling reappears in *The Words*, where Sartre tells us that his father is not even a shadow, not even a facial expression. He is nothing but a sacred parasite.

*   *   *

Fatalism is a form of negative passivity. The salvation that the Gospel speaks of is not of this type. "We shall see God," we are told. Seeing is an act. We are told that we shall inherit a

Kingdom and reign with Christ over a new land and under new skies. There is nothing passive in all this. On the contrary, it is a question of bringing about a higher kind of presence in the world, of a free obedience, of a full response to God's call, of the acquiring of a true freedom and the accession to a fullness of action. Grace impels a Christian toward the attainment of this form of superior "passivity," which by accepted obedience makes it possible to acquire an inner freedom, since Christ, who was "obedient unto death," reigns over the world of which he is the Lord.

Grace penetrates our being with the life and the power of Christ's action. This life is first of all received, and in order to receive it man has to be receptive. Man transfigured in this way is established as the king of creation, and he is able to reign effectively.

We find this dialectic of passivity and activity again in the mystery of love. Love is forgetting oneself and giving to the other. At the same time it is the reception of the other in ourselves. Marriage is the *locus* of the consummation and the fulfillment of love, its age of adulthood. When a human being allows himself to open out to another, when he agrees to come out of himself in order to enter into another's world, then he has become truly himself. Undoubtedly, *person* means to will to be one's self, but it is also the acceptance of the other's existence and of the fact that by that very existence his will is limited.

Hegel described that dialectic, especially "in regard to certain forms of religious love as they are found in Christian art: Christ's love for his disciples, the Madonna's love for her son, etc."

Love (*die Liebe*) consists in forgetting oneself in another "self" (*Selbst*) and yet also in possessing one's self precisely in this subsiding of self (*Vergehen*), in this self-forgetting (*Vergessen*). Love is a way for the person to be at home in the spirit of another. It is a return harmonized from one's other toward one's self. The other is an "other" in whom the spirit *remains*, and this is possible only because the other is a spiritual personality.[9]

In *L'Action*, Maurice Blondel perceived this concentric movement in the waves of human action. At the very moment when the action is thought to be locked within itself, to close the two excessively separated arms of the willed will and the willing will, in other words at the moment in love when man hopes to realize a kind of absolute in an instant of time—*Verweile doch! du bist so schön!* (Tarry a while, you are so beautiful!)—the circle opens again and the couple is led toward a still broader world of self-forgetfulness:

> It is done. It seems that in being bodily united to form one soul, and united by the souls to form one body, the couple have found their All. *Tenui eum nec dimittam.* And yet, when through this mysterious exchange two beings now form one more perfect being, does their mutual presence, their common action close the circle of their will? Is this full possession the terminal point where the thrust of desire ceases? No. Two beings are now one, and it is when they are one that they become three. By an action this miracle of generation marks what must be and what is the profound will of those very persons who hope to find in their unstable oneness a moment of repose, satiety, and sufficiency. . . . Thus, the will always seems to exceed itself, as if some new waves, coming from the center, were constantly pushing out the ever-widening circles of the action—the action which at every moment seems to be the ultimate perfection of a world but which is perpetually the beginning of a new world.
>
> This perpetuity that love requires, this indissoluble and surviving oneness, we find in the child. The very thrust of passion breaks the magic circle wherein it hoped it might possibly be enclosed forever. In this absolute, this sufficiency, and this eternity of one moment for which it has been unendingly seeking, the will at that very moment is already beyond itself; it wants the soul of the loved one in order to produce a body. A third being appears, as if to make up for the fruitless attempt of unity; it is no longer love, *osculum*, it is born of love; it manifests love's power and weakness; it seals it within a tomb—the cradle—and does not return what it took from its parents. They are now several and are rich. They are several, and they are poor because they are no longer one. A strange dawn has

come: during the growth process the family has to open up and part; mutual affection multiplies by dividing.

Thus the end of love is not love but the family, the first natural and necessary group where life is born and grows as in a warm bosom sheltered from the immensity of the universe.[10]

Thus, it is through the mediation of such an everyday experience as love in the heart of the family, the mutual encounter, the giving of self, that the values of salvation in communion appear.

The Old Testament used the same images to reveal the great reality of God's love to the people of Israel. The chosen people was truly the people whom God wanted to call to participate in the kingdom, if they listened to the Word and opened themselves to the divine love. This acceptance is not servility or negative passivity, but active availability, openness, and receptiveness. It is not without reason that the righteousness and holiness of the people of God are presented by the prophets Jeremiah, Ezekiel and Hosea in terms of the bride's faithfulness to the divine Bridegroom, the Bridegroom who is also the creator of the chosen people. In the same way married life serves as a model for the imagery and language of Hosea, the author of the Song of Songs, and for St. John in the Book of Revelation. Nowhere better than in this mystery of marriage can we see the juncture and the close connection of the receptive availability of love and the birth of a real personality, the true "image of God" in mankind. Christ was obedient even to the point of death. "Therefore God has highly exalted him and bestowed on him the name which is above every name. . . ."[11]

III. AVAILABILITY AND CREATIVITY

We have now reached the pivotal point of this book. Self-assertion in autonomy gives us a kind of framework for a dimension that includes both an opening out and a giving aspect. Extending the curve of human experience, we have a glimpse into the heart of its autonomy and can see there a way that could lead us along the paths of God's salvation.

True passivity is an activity of a superior kind. It is a higher form of acting. It can be understood through the artistic experience. The way a poet looks at a landscape is quite different from that of a technologist who wants to transform it: the poet recollects and admires what he sees; apparently he is passive, just as a man listening to a concert seems passive. But his passivity has nothing in common with slavery or alienation. It is an availability, an opening out to another beyond the self, a gratuitous contemplation, a higher freedom.

Man's life is inscribed within a double movement. One part is domination or the movement of being sent toward the world; from this point of view Christ is King, because he came into the world and in that world conquered sin and death. And secondly, this movement is one of acceptance and receptivity, an opening out to God for the generation of the life of grace: Christ, as Son (and we along with him, for in the depth of our souls Christ's Spirit dwells) "returns" to the Father in the communion of life received from him.

We must make modern man understand that receptivity is not opposed to freedom. On the contrary, man is free to the extent that he is "available."

To help him discover God, we must at once show him both the hidden God and the father God. We must make him become aware also of the trust God has given him in his responsibility for creation.

The face of God is uncovered in the mystical experience of rebirth into the spiritual life. Salvation is God in Jesus Christ, the grace of participating in his divine life, which has caused us to conquer death. According to Blondel's expression, then, we can be "god with God."

Thus, through the mechanics of the interior life, we find ourselves face to face with an alternative that sums up all practical teaching. On his own, man can be only what he already is despite himself, what he pretends to become voluntarily. Whatever the case, will he be willing to live, even to the point of death, so to speak, by consenting to be supplanted by God? Or will he claim to be sufficient without him, and to profit by his necessary presence without making it voluntary, borrowing from it the strength to do without

God, and desiring infinitely without desiring the infinite? To want to do something without being able to accomplish it or to have the capacity for something without the will is the choice given to us by our freedom: loving ourselves to the point of scorning God, loving God to the point of scorning ourselves. Not that this tragic contrast is so clearly and keenly obvious to everyone. But if the thought that there is something to be done with our lives is offered us, this suffices for even the coarsest among us to be called to resolve this most important matter which alone is necessary. . . .

Man's aspiration is to be a god: to be god without God and against God; to be god by God and with God is the dilemma. When we are dealing with being, and being by itself, we find that the law of contradiction applies at its strictest, and freedom is exercized to its fullest extent. . . .

The quite simple way in which the problem of destiny as a choice is popularly conceived as something quite personal to each individual, a choice between good and evil, between God's order and the drive of selfishness, is the most profound drama of the interior life.[12]

Modern man's mistrust obliges us to go thoroughly into the idea of salvation. It invites us to bear witness to holiness, and to manifest it in our own lives. We must deplore the apparent scarcity of saints but we must also understand that there exist "middle grade" saints.

We must come back to Christ who is present to the world because he is open to God. This is God's gift on which man's kingship is based. What God wills in us is the sole means of activating within our willed will the infinite aspect of the willing will.

Bergson discovered this articulation of mysticism and the presence to the world:

For the love which consumes him is no longer simply the love of man for God, it is the love of God for all men. Through God, in the strength of God, he loves all mankind

with a divine love. This is not the fraternity enjoined on us
by the philosophers in the name of reason, on the principle
that all men share by birth in one rational essence: so noble
an ideal cannot but command our respect; we may strive
to the best of our ability to put it into practice, if it be not
too irksome for the individual and the community; we shall
never attach ourselves to it passionately. Or, if we do, it
will be because we have breathed in some nook or corner
of our civilization the intoxicating fragrance left there by
mysticism. Would the philosophers themselves have laid
down so confidently the principle, so little in keeping with
everyday experience, of an equal participation of all men in
a higher essence, if there had not been mystics to embrace
all humanity in one simple indivisible love? This is not,
then, that fraternity which started as an idea, whence an
ideal has been erected. Neither is it the intensification of
an innate sympathy of man for man. Indeed we may ask
ourselves whether such an instinct ever existed elsewhere
than in the imagination of philosophers, where it was
devised for reasons of symmetry. With family, country,
humanity appearing as wider and wider circles, they thought
that man must naturally love humanity as he loves his
country and his family, whereas in reality the family group
and the social group are the only ones ordained by nature,
the only ones corresponding to instincts, and the social
instinct would be far more likely to prompt societies to
struggle against one another than to unite to make up
humanity. The utmost we can say is that family and social
feeling may chance to overflow and to operate beyond its
natural frontiers, with a kind of luxury value; it will never
go very far. The mystic love of humanity is a very different
thing. It is not the extension of an instinct, it does not
originate in an idea. It is neither of the senses nor of the
mind. It is of both, implicitly, and is effectively much
more. For such a love lies at the very root of feeling and
reason, as of all other things. Coinciding with God's love

for His handiwork, a love which has been the source of everything, it would yield up, to anyone who knew how to question it, the secret of creation. It is still more metaphysical than moral in its essence. What it wants to do, with God's help, is to complete the creation of the human species and make of humanity what it would have straightaway become, had it been able to assume its final shape without the assistance of man himself.[13]

A bit further, Bergson continues:

Has this love an object? Let us bear in mind that an emotion of a superior order is self-sufficient. Imagine a piece of music which expresses love. It is not love for any particular person. Another piece of music will express another love. Here we have two distinct emotional atmospheres, two different fragrances, and in both cases the quality of love will depend upon its essence and not upon its object. Nevertheless, it is hard to conceive a love which is, so to speak, at work, and yet applies to nothing. As a matter of fact, the mystics unanimously bear witness that God needs us, just as we need God. Why should He need us unless it be to love us? And it is to this very conclusion that the philosopher who holds to the mystical experience must come. Creation will appear to him as God undertaking to create creators, that He may have, besides Himself, beings worthy of His love.[14]

To die to oneself therefore is by no means a pursuit of the sterile purity of nothingness. It is not, as Monsieur Teste did, to turn one's soul into a desert isle. It is to allow one's self to be stripped of all ornamentation by the bridegroom, and to let one's self be "clothed" by him. It is in the superabundance of his light that our eyes are affected by the night; it is in the superabundance of his strength that we live a kind of death. It is not we who will exhaust created thought. That would be running the risk of cold sterility, as St. Teresa of Avila has said:

In mystical theology . . . the understanding no longer acts because God suspends it. . . . What I don't approve is that we presume to suspend it ourselves. Let us not put a stop to his action. If we do we shall remain cold and stupefied; frustrated both at what we had and at what we were pretending to get.[15]

This is why Teresa recommended that we never give up meditating on Jesus' earthly life.

As John of the Cross so well saw, God also empties the memory of every created image, not by denuding it in advance, but *by his very coming*, he places it in darkness through the excess of divine light. Thus the mystical bride is denuded because she is "over-dressed." John of the Cross thereby rediscovers the patristic theme of the "tunics of light":

> Since God possesses the powers and finds himself their sovereign master through their transformation in him, it is he himself who moves them and commands them in a divine way, in accordance with his divine mind and his will, so that then the operations of God and the soul are not distinct, but rather those produced by the soul are from God himself. They are divine operations insofar as, according to St. Paul's statement, he who is united to the Lord becomes one spirit with him (1 Cor. 6:17). Hence it happens that in union the operations of the soul are from the divine mind and are divine: and that these souls always produce only works that are fitting and reasonable, never works that are unfitting; the Spirit of God makes them know what they ought to know, makes them not know what it is fitting for them not to know, makes them remember what they should remember, with or without forms, makes them forget what is to be forgotten, love what they should love, and not love what is not in God. And thus, all the first movements of the powers in these souls are divine, and we should not be astonished that the movements and the operations of these powers are divine because they are transformed in the divine being.[16]

NOTES TO CHAPTER 4

1. Gabriel Marcel, *Rome n'est plus dans Rome* (Paris: Librarie Plon, 1951), p. 58.

2. *Ibid.*, p. 44.

3. *Ibid.*, p. 52.

4. *Ibid.*, pp. 49–50.

5. Franz Kafka, *Dearest Father*, trans. Ernst Kaiser and Eithne Wilkins (New York: Schocken, 1954), p. 190.

6. Gabriel Marcel, in *Existentialisme chrétien* (Paris: Librarie Plon, 1947), pp. 302–303.

7. F. Jeanson, *Sartre par lui-même* (Paris: Ed. du Seuil, 1954), pp. 116–120.

8. *Ibid.*, p. 77.

9. Quoted and paraphrased by F. Grégoire, "L'attitude hégélienne devant l'existence," in *Revue philosophique de Louvain*, 1953, p. 217.

10. Maurice Blondel, *L'Action*, 1st ed. (Paris: Alcan, 1893), pp. 257–258; 2nd ed. (Paris, 1938), II, 263–264.

11. Phil. 2:9.

12. Blondel, *L'Action*, 1893 ed., pp. 254, 356–357; cf. 1938 ed., II, 349 but in more abstract terms), 360.

13. Henri Bergson, *The Two Sources of Morality and Religion* (New York: Holt, 1935), pp. 222–223.

14. *Ibid.*, p. 243.

15. Quoted and commented upon in J. Maréchal, *Etudes sur la psychologie des Mystiques* (Bruges, 1924).

16. *Ascent of Mt. Carmel*, Bk. III, Ch. ii. This passage is quoted and commented on in J. Maritain, *The Degrees of Knowledge* (New York: Scribner's, 1959), pp. 332–333.

PART TWO

POSITIVE APPROACHES

5

A Bridge-Writer:

St.-John Perse

IN APPROACHING THE POSITIVE ASPECT OF THE PROBLEM OF SALVA-
tion, I should like to pick as a starting point the literary work
of St.-John Perse. It is poetic, yet at the same time open to the
contemporary world. There can be found the presence of the two
poles: man's domination over the world (we know its importance to the sensibilities of modern man), and that other pole
whose value must absolutely be reaffirmed—availability, receptiveness, and openness to something other than oneself, to a
personal presence that is totally accepted and received.

There are two aspects important to our presenting the doctrine of salvation: *death to the self*, in accepting of a life of God
in ourselves which crucifies us in order to make us live, to make
us rise (Blondel insisted upon this, following an Augustinian
point of view), and, secondly, *a presence to the world*, the presence of the world to man, a progress which man brings about
as the one responsible for this world. When man dies, he dies
totally to himself; but everything truly righteous and truly
charitable in his life will be found again in the "beyond" (I use
this expression for want of a better one). This is the viewpoint
of Teilhard de Chardin. Not an "other world" but a world that
is "other."

If we come to place more value on these two complementary
aspects: self-affirmation and self-openness to others, we shall

have gone a great way toward clearing the ground, at least, in modern man's attitude toward salvation.

St.-John Perse received the Nobel prize for literature in 1960. He is one of those writers, only too rare, who represent a tradition that Frenchmen of France tend sometimes to forget. This particular "France" never experienced the emaciation that Voltaire caused the country to go through in the eighteenth century. The literature of the French West Indies could serve as a bridge between the very "problematical" European literature and other literatures which may be less perfect in form but which are profoundly marked by the experience of the world's presence to man and man's presence in the world. I am thinking particularly of the French literature from black Africa. Take, for example, Léopold Senghor, president of Sénégal, who is also a great poet; Aimé Césaire, the deputy from Martinique; Rabemananjara, and a whole series of writers using French who are black. They come from Africa, the West Indies, Madagascar. Their vision of man and of the world is marked by a very simple feeling that might well inspire a new "emergent world" romanticism, one that stresses the presence of the world to man and man's presence in the world in a vital communication.

An enquiry addressed recently to twenty-two black French writers showed that practically none of them (with the exception of Frantz Fanon, deputy and writer from North Africa) had been influenced by existentialism and the problematical literature which we have treated in the first part of this essay. In their literature, the individual problem of love, of loneliness, is left in the shadows. Senghor has frequently stated that when a black man in one of his novels says "I"—and that is quite rare— it always means "we." The blacks judge that our European literature is much too problematical and that our writers are in the process of sawing off the branch on which they are sitting.[1]

A writer like St.-John Perse, born on Guadeloupe, sets up a bridge. The universe he shows us in his poetry is inspired by a certain number of themes from contemporary French literature, for example surrealism, the style of Francis Jammes, possibly some Claudel, but at the same time he is connected with the lyrical tradition of presence in the world, in space and time, which is characteristic of African literature.

His first collections of poems, especially, speak of this marriage bond with the universe. They will give us the key to this second section on the positive approaches to salvation. Here the poet speaks of his childhood:

Palms . . . !
In those days they bathed you in water-of green-leaves; and the water was of green sun too; and your mother's maids, tall glistening girls, moved their warm legs near you who trembled . . .
(I speak of a high condition, in those days, among the dresses, in the dominion of revolving lights.)

Palms! and the sweetness
of an aging of roots . . . ! the earth
in those days longed to be deafer, and deeper the sky where trees too tall, weary of an obscure design, knotted an inextricable pact . . .
(I dreamed this dream, in esteem: a safe sojourn among enthusiastic linens.)

. . . .

In those days, men's mouths
were more grave, women's arms moved more slowly; in those days, feeding like us on roots, great silent beasts were ennobled;
and longer over darker shadow eyelids were lifted . . .
(I dreamed this dream, it has consumed us without relics.)[2]

Praise bursts out in a simple hymn:

And my mother's maids, tall glistening girls . . . And our fabulous eyelids . . . O
radiance! O favours!
Naming each thing, I proclaimed that it was great, naming each beast, that it was beautiful and good.[3]

This "naming" of all things to say that they are good reminds us of Genesis, where Adam appears as king of creation. The Prince theme is constantly to be found in Perse's work, along with the theme of praise:

(. . . O I have cause to praise! O bountiful fable, O table of abundance!)[4]

Such is the way of the world and I have nothing but good to say of it. . . .[5]

Into this world of communion, his father appears:

Palms!
and on the crackling house such spears of fire!
. . . The voices were a bright noise on the wind . . . Reverently, my father's boat brought tall white forms: really, wind-blown angels perhaps; or else wholesome men dressed in good linen with pith helmets (like my father, who was noble and seemly).[6]

And his mother:

. . . How beautiful your mother was, how pale,
when so tall and so languid, stooping,
she straightened your heavy hat of straw or of sun, lined with a double seguine leaf,
and when, piercing a dream to shadows consecrated, the dazzle of muslin
inundated your sleep![7]

Childhood is brought up with the freshness of early morning:

Childhood, my love, was it only that? . . .
Childhood, my love . . . that double ring of the eye and the ease of loving . . .
It is too calm and then so warm,
so continuous too,
that it is strange to be there, hands plunged in the facility of day . . .[8]

The ease of loving: how can this fail to remind us of Camus's gradual and painful discovery of the difficulty of loving? The ease of loving, which is related to that mysterious bond that binds the sleeping person on his couch to the tide, to the sea beyond, which is turning back:

It is a bit after midnight, at the time of great opaqueness; see how, in sleep, one whose breathing is bound to the breathing of the sea and to the turn of the tide, see how he turns on his bed like a ship changing its tack of sail.[9]

The ease of loving is shown in a paternal and serene world:

Palms! and the sweetness
of an aging of roots! . . . the breath of the trade winds,
wild doves and the feral cat
piercing the bitter foliage where, in the rawness of an
evening with an odour of Deluge,
moons, rose and green, were hanging like mangoes.

*

. . . And the Uncles in low voices talked with my mother. They had hitched their horses at the gate. And the House endured under the plumed trees.[10]

As curious as it might seem, this recalls those evenings at Combray at the beginning of Proust's *Remembrance of Things Past*, when the little bell in the leaves near the grill announced the arrival of Charles Swann. There too the house perdured beneath the trees of the Ile de France.

Thus, from one world to another, bonds are formed and reformed. They are poetic and human, the only true bonds.

*   *   *

St.-John Perse also sings of the heartbreak of the city-dweller cut off from virgin nature which is alive and recreates, being like the hard ground that restored Antaeus' strength. He has said this in the Robinson Crusoe poems, for example in "The City":

Slate covers the roofs, or else tiles where mosses grow.
Their breath flows out through the chimneys.
Grease!
Odour of men in crowds, like the stale smell of a slaughter-house! sour bodies of women under their skirts!

O City against the sky!

Grease! breaths rebreathed, and the smoke of a polluted people—for every city encompasses filth.

On the dormer-window of the little shop—on the garbage cans of the poor-house—on the odour of cheap wine in the sailors' quarter—on the fountain sobbing in the police courtyards—on the statues of mouldy stone and on stray dogs—on the little boy whistling, and the beggar whose cheeks tremble in the hollow of his jaws,

on the sick cat with three wrinkles on its forehead,

the evening descends, in the smoke of men . . .

—The City like an abscess flows through the river to the sea . . .

Crusoe!—this evening over your Island, the sky drawing near will give praise to the sea, and the silence will multiply the exclamation of the solitary stars.

Draw the curtains, do not light the lamp:

It is evening on your Island and all around, here and there, wherever arches the faultless vase of the sea; it is evening the colour of eyelids, on the roads woven of sky and of sea.

Everything is salty, everything is viscous and heavy like the life of plasmas.

The bird rocks itself in its feathers, in an oily dream; the hollow fruit, deafened by insects, falls into the water of the creeks, probing its noise.

The island falls asleep in the arena of vast waters, washed by warm currents and unctuous milt, in the embrace of sumptuous slime.

Under the propagating mangroves, slow fishes in the mud have discharged bubbles with their flat heads; and others that are slow, spotted like reptiles, keep watch.—The slime is fecundated—Hear the hollow creatures rattling in their shells—Against a bit of green sky there is a sudden puff of smoke which is the tangled flight of mosquitoes—The

crickets under the leaves are gently calling to each other—
And other gentle creatures, heedful of the night, sing a
song purer than the signs of the coming rains: it is the swal-
lowing of two pearls swelling their yellow gullets . . .

Wailing of waters swirling and luminous!

Corollas, mouths of watered silks: mourning that breaks
and blossoms! Big moving flowers on a journey, flowers alive
forever, and that will not cease to grow throughout the
world . . .

O the colour of the winds circling over the calm waters,
the palm-leaves of the palm-trees that stir!

And no distant barking of a single dog that means a hut;
and means a hut and the evening smoke and the three black
stones under the odour of pimentoes.

But the bats stipple the soft evening with little cries.

Joy! O joy set free in the heights of the sky!

. . . Crusoe! you are there! and your face is proffered to
the signs of the night like an upturned palm.[11]

In the human being St.-John Perse has always emphasized
those two complementary aspects about which we have already
spoken. Man as a prince is the theme at the center of a poem
called *Anabasis*. In his process of conquering, the prince comes
to a very ancient desert country on the Asian plateau in the
heart of China. St.-John Perse speaks of his "horse soul" to
evince the strength of his statement. Here he connects with
symbols from Hamitic literature, examples of which we can find
in the culture of Rwanda-Burundi. But man is also a being open
to something other than himself. The poem speaks also of man's
soul as being a young woman gone mad with grace. The prince
is also a being-in-communion, in communication with the forces
of nature, with poetic inspiration, represented by the figure of
the moving tuft of grass, taken up by the movement of the
wind. We have here a figure of man in which the two poles are
balanced.

The one who spoke of his "horse's soul" is evidently also "the
Prince beneath the tuft of grass," and the "Story-Teller at the
foot of the turpentine tree":

. . . ha! all sorts of men in their ways and fashions; and of a sudden! behold in his evening robes and summarily settling in turn all questions of precedence, the Story-Teller who stations himself at the foot of the turpentine tree . . .[12]

The prince remains among the people:

. . . So I haunted the City of your dreams, and I established in the desolate markets the pure commerce of my soul, among you
invisible and insistent as a fire of thorns in the gale.[13]

In the "Song" that begins *Anabasis*, the soul appears as a "young woman gone mad with grace":

"Hail, daughter! under the most considerable trees of the year."
. . . "My Soul, great girl, you had your ways which are not ours."
. . ."Hail, daughter! robed in the loveliest robe of the year."[14]

*   *   *

It is interesting to note that this polarity of the masculine and feminine element is found again in the vision of history in both time and space. Throughout his whole work we find a balance from one pole to the other. The poem *Winds*, one of his most beautiful works, even though it is quite hard to understand and requires a sort of detailed exegesis, is in the last analysis a poem of the new world. St.-John Perse was exiled from France. As Briand's secretary before the ascendancy of Paul Reynaud, he was practically *the* man of the French Foreign Office, and the French diplomat most hated by the Third Reich. In June of 1940, deprived of all rights of French citizenship, he went into exile in the United States. He had lost everything and was separated from his mother who was to die during his exile.

Instead of nurturing a bitterness for the old continent of Europe—his family had left in the eighteenth century and in his youth he had returned to his lycée and university studies—

he always maintained that the new world needed to keep its ties to the old. Forced to enter this new world, which became his new homeland, St.-John Perse tried to understand it. In *Winds,* he showed the complexity of the American, who is always turned to the West, to the Pacific, to discover, conquer and transform the world, but who at the same time is fascinated by the South, where dreams and contemplation dominate.

Onto this image he grafted other aspects: the thrust of industry, civilizations and their death. But instead of this vision inspiring pessimism in him, and instead of his giving in to a kind of fatalism, in the manner of Paul Valéry he supports a tonic affirmation of human values, still involving these two themes: man is prince, and man must remain open to something which is other than himself.

A few quotes will illustrate this vision of a "modern" world that is new, unsafe, violent and threatened:

> These were very great winds over all the faces of this world,
>
> Very great winds rejoicing over the world, having nor eyrie nor resting-place,
>
> Having nor care nor caution, and leaving us, in their wake,
>
> Men of straw in the year of straw . . . Ah, yes, very great winds over all the faces of the living![15]

The fleeting face of earth is recalled in the great sweeping away of cultures and "the tomes are in their niches, liked stuffed animals under wrappings, long ago, in their jars within the closed rooms of the great Temples—the tomes, innumerable and sad, in high cretaceous strata carrying credence and sediment through the ascent of time. . . ."[16] The "new" world (only here what is meant is the world of the U.S.A.), faced with the too tired wisdom of Europe, is conjured up in this fine passage:

> New lands, out there, in their very lofty perfume of humus and foliage,
>
> New lands, out there, beneath the lengthening of this world's most expansive shadows,

All the land of trees, out there, its background of black vines, like a Bible of shadow and freshness in the unrolling of this world's most beautiful texts.

And once more there is birth of prodigious things, freshness and source of freshness on the brow of man, the immemorial.

And there is a taste of things anterior, like the evocation of sources and commentaries for the great preliminary Titles,

Like the great prefatory pages for the great Books of Maecenas—the Dedication to the Prince, and the Foreword, and the Authority's Introduction.

New lands, up there, like a powerful perfume of tall women ripening,

New lands, up there, beneath the ascent of men of every age, singing the signal misalliance,

All the land of trees, up there, in the swaying of its most beautiful shades, opening the blackest of its tresses and the imposing ornament of its plumage, like a perfume of flesh, nubile and vigorous, in the bed of this world's most beautiful beings.

And there is a freshness of free waters, of shades, for the ascent of men of every age, singing the signal misalliance,

And there is a freshness of lands in infancy, like a perfume of things everlasting, on this side of everlasting things,

And like a prenuptial dream wherein man, on the verge of another age, retains his rank, interpreting the black leaf and the arborescences of silence in vaster syllabaries.

All the land, up there, new beneath its blazonry of storm, wearing the crest of golden girls and the feathered headdress of the Sachem,

All the nubile and vigorous land, in the steps of the Stranger, opening up the fable of its grandeur to the dreams and pageantries of another age.

And the land in its long lines, on its longest strophes, running, from sea to sea, to loftier scriptures, in the distant unrolling of this world's most beautiful texts.

*

Thither were we going, westward-faced, to the roaring of new waters. And once more there is birth of prodigious things in the land of men. And all your painted birds are not enough. O Audubon, but I must needs add unto them some species now extinct: the Passenger-Pigeon, the Northern Curlew, and the Great Auk . . .

Thither we were going, from swell to swell, along the Western degrees. And, from the outskirts of the cities toward the stubble-fields, amidst the freckled flesh of women of the open air, the night was fragrant with the black salts of the land. And the women were tall, with the taste of citrus and rye, and of wheat seeds moulded in the image of their bodies.

And from you, O girls, at the doors of the halls, we ravished that continuous stir of evening in your free-breathing hair—all that odour of heat and dryness, your aura, like a flash of light from elsewhere . . . And your legs were long and like those that surprise us in dreams, on the sands, in the lengthening out of the day's last rays . . . Night, singing among the rolling-mills of the cities, draws forth no purer cipher for the ironwork of very lofty style.

And who, then, has been to sleep this night? The great expresses have gone by, hastening to the chasms of another age, with their supply of ice for five days. They were running against the wind, strapped with white metal, like aging athletes. And, on their cries, so many airplanes gave chase! . . .

Let the rivers in their risings multiply! And the roads that go rocketing upwards hold us breathless! . . . The one-way Cities haul their loads to the open roads. And once more there is a rush of new girls to the New Year, wearing, under the nylon, the fresh almond of their sex.

And there are messages on every wire, marvels on every wave. And in this same movement, to all this movement joined, my poem, continuing in the wind, from city to city and river to river, flows onward with the highest waves of the earth, themselves wives and daughters of other waves . . .[17]

Then this cry bursts out, called forth by the whole poem:

. . . But man is in question! So when will it be a question of man himself?—Will someone in the world raise his voice?

For man is in question, in his human presence; and the eye's enlargement over the loftiest inner seas.

. . . .

For man is in question, and his reintegration.

Will no one in the world raise his voice? Testimony for man . . .[18]

Finally the wind theme returns. The winds are enriched, quelled, and become constructive:

. . . These were very great winds over the land of men— very great winds at work among us,

Singing to us the horror of living, and singing to us the honour of living, ah! singing to us and singing to us from the very summit of peril,

And, with the savage flutes of misfortune, leading us, new men, to our new ways.

These were very great forces at work on the causeway of men—very great forces in labour

Holding us outside of custom and holding us outside of season, among men of custom, among men of season,

And on the savage stone of misfortune stripping bare for us the land that is vintaged for new nuptials.[19]

Swept away by a cosmic maelstrom, successive civilizations disappear one after the other, leaving but a few traces. In the eye of this maelstrom, this cosmic whirlpool (for the primordial image is one of oceans and water) St.-John Perse shows us the extremely close and at the same time extremely fragile connection between a man and a woman in love. In *Amers* there is a lengthy song, entitled: *Étroits sont les vaisseaux*. The woman's body is like a narrow ship. The love that joins the man and the woman in a connection that is at once very close and very fragile is bound up with the eternal becoming, the *Tao* of the Chinese, with the eternal movement of death and resurrection that constitutes life. The lover knows that when the rain begins to fall on the roof of the room in which he has been with the woman, he will get up to go to his work, become an exile again with his soul of a prince, of a conqueror, a transformer of the world. The ship image is followed by the figure of ports, symbols of departure.

> . . . Laid at your side, like the car in the bottom of the boat; rolled at your side, like the sail with the yard, lashed at the foot of the mast . . .
>
> . . . Go more gently, O course of things to their end. . . . The salty night bears us in its flanks.
>
> . . . And the Woman who loves fans her eyelashes in all this very great calm. The level sea surrounds me and opens for me the fronds of its palms. . . . And my lip is salty with the salt of my birth and your body is salty with the salt of my birth . . . You are here, my love, and I have no place to save in you.[20]

At the summit of his published work to date we have a grasp of why, when St.-John Perse speaks of growing old, he leaves aside childhood nostalgia and does not speak of the years of old age, but rather: "Great age! we are here." From exile to renewal, the poet of *Chronique* knows that he must be concerned not with the past but with the future. André Rousseaux has written that although he does not give full religious meaning to the word soul, he orients it still less in the direction of what the word *psyche* can mean psychologically. The soul is the attribute of the Master:

> For us, already, a song of higher adventure. The road
> traced by a new hand, and fires carried from crest to
> crest . . .
> But a graver song, of another steel, like a song of honour
> and great age and a song of the Master, alone in the even-
> ing, forging his way, before the hearthfire
> —pride of the soul before the soul and pride of soul grow-
> ing to greatness in the great blue sword.[21]

In this lyrical description of a man and a woman, there is
a preciseness of language and a nobility in the art of connecting
this love to the movement of the waves, which makes this poem
one of the most beautiful French poems of the twentieth
century.

Undoubtedly the ship is in the eye of the maelstrom. The
man always leaves the woman. This love is an ephemeral one.
But St.-John Perse, in showing us a true man who is prince
over the world but also joined to the world, and in hymning
the love of the man and woman in the center of this great
movement that carries everyone off toward death, puts us in a
climate of truth and life. His work is not Christian, but neither
is it anti-Christian. It is an evocation of some of the rhythms
of the world, both positive and negative, masculine and feminine, joining and separation, departure and return. He is a kind
of "secular" Claudel.

The Bible reminds us that civilizations succeed one another
and that none is immortal. God leads history along in his own
way, which is not our way and we cannot know it. But what we
do on earth has positive value when we live in righteousness
and love.

The world unfolded by St.-John Perse is virginal. It is unstable
and shaky, strong and weak. It is *nubile*, ready for marriage,
beyond the plans of individuals and particular generations. The
instability of this world, which *Winds* makes almost tangible, is
revealed in the Bible. But we know that the mysterious stability
of the world, like the stability of the mountains, rests on the
promise of God; the Spirit has roused our decrepit wisdom, only
to dissolve and recompose it. "There were great winds over the
whole face of the earth," the poet has told us, and the Gospel
answers: "The wind blows where it wills, and you hear the

sound of it, but you do not know whence it comes or whither it goes; so it is with everyone who is born of the Spirit."[22]

This poetry, which is so exact and has such preciseness that it reminds us of the exactness of science, is also so lyrical that it makes us think of the sacred books of India. But it can also be the heart's delight of the pedant who will rejoice in "explaining" it with the lyricism of a dictionary. He will not, however, be able to continue for very long. Through a violently opened window will come the breeze of the world itself, and it will carry off all his dictionary jottings toward that mysterious Living Being about whom St.-John Perse has said: "You are my promise in the East, and this promise will be kept upon the sea."

NOTES TO CHAPTER 5

1. Read Lilyan Kesteloot, *Les Ecrivians noirs de langue française* (Brussels: Ed. Institut Solvay, 1963).

2. St.-John Perse, "To Celebrate a Childhood," *Eloges and Other Poems*, trans. Louise Varèse, rev. ed., Bollingen Series LV (New York: Pantheon, 1956), pp. 7, 9.

3. *Ibid.*, p. 9.

4. *Ibid.*, p. 19.

5. St.-John Perse, *Anabasis*, trans T. S. Eliot, rev. ed. (New York: Harcourt, 1949), p. 41.

6. "To Celebrate a Childhood," *Eloges*, p. 19.

7. *Ibid.*, p. 15.

8. "Praises," *Eloges*, pp. 27, 29.

9. St.-John Perse, *Oeuvre poétique*, I (Paris: Gallimard, 1960), p. 222.

10. "To Celebrate a Childhood," *Eloges*, p. 21.

11. "Pictures for Crusoe: The City," *Eloges*, pp. 53, 55, 57.

12. *Anabasis*, p. 85.

13. *Ibid.*, p. 27.

14. *Ibid.*, pp. 19, 21.

15. St.-John Perse, *Winds*, trans. Hugh Chisholm, 2nd ed., Bollingen Series XXXIV (New York: Pantheon, 1961), p. 5.

16. *Ibid.*, p. 21.

17. *Ibid.*, pp. 51, 53, 55.

18. *Ibid.*, pp. 113, 119.

19. *Ibid*, p. 179.

20. St.-John Perse, *Seamarks*, trans. Wallace Fowlie, Bollingen Series LXVII (New York: Pantheon, 1958), pp. 137, 139.

21. St.-John Perse, *Chronique*, trans. Robert Fitzgerald, Bollingen Series LXIX (New York: Pantheon, 1961), p. 47.

22. John 3:8.

6

Personal Salvation

I. LITERATURE THAT IS NOT "FOR EVERYONE"

AS FATHER BLANCHET ONCE REMARKED, WE HAVE A CHRISTIAN literature today that is not meant for universal consumption.[1]

At one time, it was possible to distinguish a Catholic novel from one that was not. The Catholic novelist followed—or pretended to follow—a set of "rules." The man who did not observe a certain number of these rules became a sort of road hog—the man who does not follow the rules of the road is soon noticed.

However, present-day Christian literature (take Julian Green, Graham Greene, Bernanos, and Mauriac, for example) is at the very opposite end of the spectrum.

In Graham Greene's *The Heart of the Matter*, Scobie is married. He is unfaithful to his wife with a pretty girl whom he saved from a shipwreck. He does not succeed in choosing between them, because he feels that if he abandons the girl she will despair and kill herself. If he tries to make her understand that he must leave her because he is married and must be faithful to his wife, she will not understand. She will merely say that he does not love her any more. To resolve the problem he kills himself, making it seem like an accident. His last words are "Dear God, I love." This leaves us with a certain ambiguity. Does he mean: "Dear God, I did love and this is my only chance for heaven," or : "It is You whom I love ultimately"? In an interview published in *Dieu Vivant*, Graham Greene explained that the ambiguity was intentional.[2] When Scobie's wife, Louise, finds out about her husband's suicide she says to

97

Father Rank, the priest in the novel, that Scobie is damned. The priest answers that she has absolutely no idea what the love of God is. What Greene wants to show is that someone who is apparently damned has probably the greatest chance for being saved, while Louise, who is surest of salvation, is actually running the risk of not being saved at all.

> "And at the end, this—horror. He must have known that he was damning himself."
>
> "Yes, he knew that all right. He never had any trust in mercy—except for other people."
>
> "It's no good even praying. . . ."
>
> Father Rank clapped the cover of the diary to and said furiously, "For goodness' sake, Mrs. Scobie, don't imagine you—or I— know a thing about God's mercy."
>
> "The Church says. . . ."
>
> "I know the Church says. The Church knows all the rules. But it doesn't know what goes on in a single human heart."
>
> "You think there's some hope then?" she wearily asked.
>
> "Are you so bitter against him?"
>
> "I haven't any bitterness left."
>
> "And do you think God's likely to be more bitter than a woman?" he said with harsh insistence, but she winced away from the arguments of hope.
>
> "Oh why, why, did he have to make such a mess of things?"
>
> Father Rank said, "It may seem an odd thing to say— when a man's as wrong as he was—but I think, from what I saw of him, that he really loved God."[3]

François Mauriac had already taken some steps along this road. In *Vipers' Tangle* respectable people are pharisaical. If they remain so they have little chance of reaching their goal in the "beyond." On the other hand, Louis, who was converted late in life, had always been closer to God even though he never suspected it himself.

Salvation is a *personal* encounter with God, the love of neighbor in God. No one may judge in God's place. Between the stirrup and the ground, "between the bridge and the water" as the Curé d'Ars used to say, much can happen.

Only God is judge. To recall the mystery of the dialogue between God and sinful man is extremely important, but only if we do not go to the other extreme and say that the only serious Christian novel is one of this type. In the works of Bourget and Barrès, for example, there is a great deal that is interesting.

II. BALZACIAN SOCIETY AND SALVATION

In this kind of personalist literature there are two tendencies.

The emulators of Balzac, faithful to the master's technique, describe a certain society from a very specific cultural and economic point of view. Within this society they present the religious problem. Mauriac is "Balzacian" in an entire aspect of his work. He introduced the province of Bordeaux into French literature. The characters and families he describes are sociologically very individualized. We should be able to pick them out in a crowd, and it is within this context that Mauriac presents the problem of salvation or damnation. In *Vipers' Tangle*, for example, the old man is a rich and miserly landowner. We know exactly how many vines he has. When a storm breaks out one night and it begins to hail, he rushes to the particular vineyard which produces the most expensive wine in order to protect it with a piece of cloth. In the morning he is found stretched out on the ground like a fragile rampart between the storm and the vine. But at the same time, because of the singularity of this individual and the family that surrounds him we have a drama of salvation, to which we shall return.

Alongside this "Balzacian technique," there is a type of literature in which this sociological aspect is short-circuited, so to speak, by the lightning of grace. The only drama in Bernanos and Julian Green is the supernatural drama, the combat between God and Satan in man's heart. With Bernanos the sociological side merely serves as a background. In *Diary of a Country Priest*, the château is like dozens of others in France and Belgium. Similarly, the peasant village with its low houses glued together and its fertile, rich clay soil reminds us also of the farms of Flanders. The characters are affected only by the drama Bernanos describes, the combat between God and evil: "Between Satan and God, God has placed only the heart of man."

There are two tendencies, then, in this literature: one is in a sociological frameword, with Mauriac, and to a certain extent Graham Greene, who always mingles his description of the spiritual drama with a critique of Anglo-Saxon civilization, where he pays special attention to its hypocritical character. The other leaves this sociological, cultural and economic aspect aside, to the point that all that remains is the spiritual drama.

III. MEDIATION OF OTHERS

In the literature we are treating, the characters are sinful to the extent that they believe they are not loved. In *Vipers' Tangle* this is very striking. The miserly old man, whose children call him "the old crocodile," had believed for a long time that nobody loved him, that his daughters were always making fun of him. In his youth he was quite struck when his fiancée, Isa, had told him that she had never seen a young man with such long eyelashes. But one night, absent-mindedly, his wife betrayed the secret of her life: she had married him only because whe was afraid of being an old maid. This caused him to fall apart. From then on he embittered his wound and fashioned a "time-bomb" for his heirs: when they open his will, they see that he has disinherited every one of them. Mauriac takes great care in describing the steps of this revenge.

Very simple events bring about a flaw in his hard-heartedness. The man was disliked by his family. He was a miser and spoke little. He had mistresses, no longer went to mass; from his bed he heard the children asking what Sunday after Pentecost it was. But his youngest daughter liked to come and sit on his lap, say good-morning to him, and pray for him. This was the first touch of love on his withered heart. Another time it was a priest who had been engaged as tutor for his children at Malagar, near Bordeaux. The young priest was in bad odor with his bishop for having gone to the opera. Very happy at being welcomed into this house for two months of vacation (for he had his board and gave a few lessons to the children) he opened up to the old man, explaining his own insignificant clerical difficulties and adding: "Ah, Monsieur, you are kind." The old man began to laugh, saying that the young priest had no idea how comical his words were, since in his family and his surroundings no one thought of him as a kind person. The old man was bothered by what the priest had told him. Lastly, his nephew, Luc, a practicing Christian, was always full of kindness toward him and showed him the same fondness he extended to the others. Luc was called into the army and sent the old man a card which he signed "Fondly." In reading this word, the old man told himself that had things been different he might have received the same thing from his own child.

These glimpses of the love people have for him he finds distressing. What we are looking for is to be loved not despite the fact that we are sinners and unworthy, but precisely *because* we are unworthy, because we are sinners. We ask that people love us as we are, not as accomplices in our weaknesses, but in order that we might be forgiven and given back hope and life.

These barely visible marks of friendship and tenderness that people give him, even though he does not deserve them, gradually forge a wedge in his heart. They detach him ever so slightly from the riches with which he identifies himself. When one night a frightful storm breaks out, threatening to destroy a vineyard, instead of throwing himself on the ground as he had done before, the old man feels suddenly detached:

> But tonight—here I am, become a stranger to what used to be, in the deepest sense, my virtue. At last I am detached. I do not know what, I do not know who, has detached me, Isa, but the cables are broken: I am drifting.
>
> What force is drawing me? A blind force? Love? Perhaps love. . . .[4]

In the autumn of his life, after his wife's death, practically alone, he comes little by little to see that he is not identified with his hatred. There is something deeper in him that seeks to be loved:

> I felt, I saw, I had it in my hands—that crime of mine. It did not consist entirely in that hideous nest of vipers— hatred of my children, desire for revenge, love of money;

but also in my refusal to seek beyond those entangled vipers. I had held fast to that loathsome tangle as though it were my very heart—as though the beatings of that heart had merged into those writhing reptiles.

It had not been enough for me, throughout half a century, to recognize nothing in myself except that which was not I. I had done the same thing in the case of other people. Those miserable greeds visible in my children's faces had fascinated me. Robert's stupidity had been what struck me about him, and I had confined myself to that superficial feature. Never had the appearance of other people presented itself to me as something that must be broken through, something that must be penetrated, before one could reach them.

It was at the age of thirty, or at the age of forty, that I should have made this discovery. But to-day I am an old man with a heart that beats too slowly, and I watch the last autumn of my life putting the vines to sleep, stupefying them with smoke and sunshine.

Those whom I should have loved are dead. Dead are those who might have loved me. As for the survivors, I no longer have the time, or the strength, to set out on a voyage towards them, to discover them. There is nothing in me, down to my voice, my gestures, my laugh, which does not belong to the monster whom I set up against the world, and to whom I gave my name.[5]

The old man sees, however, that the secret of salvation is love:

Even the elect do not learn to love all by themselves. To get beyond the absurdities, the failings, and above all the stupidity of people, one must possess a secret of love which the world has forgotten. So long as this secret is not rediscovered, you will change human conditions in vain.

I thought that it was selfishness which made me aloof from everything that concerns the economic and the social;

and it is true that I was a monster of solitude and indifference; but there was also in me a feeling, an obscure certi-
tude, that all this serves for nothing to revolutionise the
face of the world. The world must be touched at its heart.
I seek Him Who alone can achieve that victory; and He
must Himself be the Heart of hearts, the burning centre
of all love.

I felt a desire which perhaps was in itself a prayer.[6]

When he tries to talk to his granddaughter Janine, to tell her
what he has come to discover, he comes up against the distrust
of a person of habit, who fulfills her religious obligations but
who wants to go no further:

It was precisely what I had execrated all my life—just that,
nothing but that. In this crude caricature, this mean parody
of the Christian life, I had pretended to find an authentic
representation to justify me in hating it.

One must have the courage to look at what one hates
straight in the face. But I, I said to myself, I . . . Did I
not know already that I was deceiving myself, that evening
at the end of the last century on the terrace at Calèse, when
Abbé Ardouin said to me: "You are very good . . ."? Later,
I had closed my ears to the words of Marie, as she lay dying.

But, at that bedside, the secret of life and death had
been revealed to me. A little girl was dying for me. . . . I
had tried to forget. Tirelessly I had sought to lose that key
which some mysterious hand always gave back to me, at
every turning point in my life—the way Luc looked after
Mass, those Sunday mornings, at the hour of the first grass-
hopper. . . . And this spring again, the night of the hail. . . .

So my thoughts ran, that evening. I remember that I got
up, pushing my chair back so violently that Janine started.

The silence of Calèse, at that advanced hour, that thick,
almost solid silence, benumbed, stifled her grief. She let
the fire die down; and, as the room grew colder, she drew

her chair closer and closer to the hearth, until her feet almost touched the ashes. The dying fire drew her hands, her face, towards it. The lamp on the mantel-piece shed its rays upon that heavy, hunched-up woman; and I stumbled about, in the darkness encumbered with mahogany and rosewood. I hovered, impotently, around that lump of humanity, that prostrate body.

"My child. . . ." I could not find the word I sought. That which stifles me, to-night, even as I write these lines; that which makes my heart hurt as though it were going to burst; that love of which, at last, I know the name ador—[7]

How could we now mistake the meaning of the epigraph, taken from St. Teresa of Ávila, which Mauriac put at the beginning of his excellent book:

Lord, consider that we do not understand ourselves and that we do not know what we would, and that we go infinitely far astray from that which we desire.[8]

There is a certain self-knowledge of our sinfulness that it is impossible to face except before God. We cannot know ourselves as sinners except in kneeling before God. This "kneeling before God," Mauriac tells us, we attain through love for others. The central image of Mauriac's universe is the desert of love. What all of us seek is to be loved since we are unworthy.

Undoubtedly, the context here is Mauriac's. It is expressed in images that are olfactory and auditory before they become visual. Mauriac succeeds in translating spiritual realities into the most "fleshly" language, in the sense understood by Péguy. But the idea itself is universally valid and we see it again in other Christian writers, for example with Julian Green.

"Each man in his darkness goes off in search of light" is a quote from Victor Hugo. Julian Green took the first half of it as a title for a novel. His hero, Wilfred, is inhabited by a kind of wild hunger for the pleasures of the flesh, but he has never loved. He has never heard anyone tell him "I love you." When he meets a love which is even an impossible one he discovers God's love for him, which ultimately saves him.

IV. THE OPERATION OF GRACE

We must not look upon grace as a kind of ray coming out of a half-open heaven in order to surround the head of the sinner with a halo. Grace makes use of the psychological mechanism found in each of us. We are much more profoundly wicked, and much closer to God than we imagine. Or rather God is close to us and we do not know it. One scene from Julian Green's *Each in His Darkness* shows it. Wilfred is the only Catholic in his family along with his uncle Horace. He is attractive and handsome, and awakens in a certain number of people who meet him—whether men or women—a love that is sometimes una-vowable. At the same time his face radiates a kind of faith and religious peace. As someone has remarked, God, God's divine grace has never been intermingled with physical grace in such an intimate and daring manner as in this novel.

Wilfred is called to his uncle Horace. The uncle has led quite a life. He has had mistresses, is rich and has an estate in the country. He wants to see his nephew before he dies. He has lost the faith and tells Wilfred that he is afraid of dying because he no longer believes. Wilfred feels trapped and answers that he is not the one to speak to him about such matters. There is no doubt about Wilfred's faith, but at the same time he is ravaged by the passions of the flesh. He reminds his uncle that a Father Dolan will be coming to see him. But it is as if his uncle does not believe him when the priest speaks about the faith. He tells Wilfred that although he himself no longer has faith, Wilfred should pray that his faith return in order that he might die with faith. Then Wilfred answers him abruptly, saying that we *know* we have the faith just as we know that we are in love.

He says these words without thinking, but they evidently strike his uncle forcefully, since he replies by saying that Wil-fred's very words prove that he has the faith. Wilfred sees suddenly that by saying what he did to be of help to the dying man who is his uncle, he has involved himself to an extent infinitely greater than he would have consciously wished. Some-thing stirs deep within him. It happened through an unthinking moment in a sudden burst of charity toward his uncle, and has led him to a point where he had not wished to go.

His uncle pleads with him to pray that he might believe again, but Wilfred protests that he is not a saint and therefore cannot. He feels that he should, that something has snapped and broken deep inside. He falls on his knees at the foot of his uncle's bed and cries out: "Oh God, we are going to die" (the "we" is his uncle and himself). At that moment he becomes somehow part of his uncle's fate. He makes it his own and takes it on himself, and it is precisely because he takes it on himself and in a certain way accepts dying with his uncle that he says: "We are going to die and we don't have the faith, we are incapable of having the faith" (which is true, it is a grace from God). At that moment, he has the impression of rediscovering the universe in a beauty that he never noticed before. He knows that his uncle has regained his faith and that he will die with it.

Soon afterward, under the dark trees that line the river in the middle of the park, Wilfred has a kind of experience of the love of God:

> He went out and began running across the lawn till he had reached the trees above the river. Night was falling. No one could see him and he breathed in the pure sharp air with an animal joy that made him want to cry out like a child. If Angus had been there, he thought, he would have dared him to a race in the avenue that ran along the riverside. A few minutes went by before he grew calmer. Everything around him was still and, as though he wished to break the spell of this stillness, he picked up a dead twig and snapped it in two, but the huge silence closed over the little crack, sharp as a pistol shot, enveloping his hands, his head, his shoulders and his whole being. Three yards below him, the immense river rolled water that smelt of mud to the ocean, but this evening the presence of that vast and shifting expanse could only be guessed at.
>
> He sat on the grass and felt the trunk of one of the big maples that lined the avenue. By a trick of imagination that he often indulged in he pictured the trees as live beings who were watching over him. A delightful feeling of safety came over him and he lay down on his back. Now they

could knock at the door of his room, look for him: death would not find him. Clasping his hands under his neck, he let his eyes wander far away into the sky that was visible through the rents in the foliage and suddenly it seemed to him that he was in love. With whom, he could not have said, but his heart contained so much love that there was enough there, he thought, for an entire life-time. Yet it was someone he did not know that he loved with all his might. Eyes closed, he murmured with extraordinary ardour: "I love you!" The words seemed to free him from a mysterious burden and the little sentence hovered on his lips over and over again. He had never spoken it to anyone in that way and he had no one to say it to, but he said it and said it again with a strange, a new-found happiness. He fell asleep, unawares.[9]

It is in contact with others that grace lives and relives in us, in order to "go out" to others and help them. Grace can act deep within ourselves without our suspecting it. The only thing asked of us is that we not say "no," that we accept that God profit from these instants of "less bad will," these instants where love begins. Wilfred was never able to cause others pain. And it is this that will ultimately save him. He is incapable of saying "no" to others, incapable of writing someone off definitively. Since he is thus bound to others he will be led much farther than he ever imagined.

For this reason he cannot find peace of heart unless he asks forgiveness from Max, an unfortunate soul poisoned by drink. He awakens in him the clear hatred of one who knows that love exists and that he has been unfaithful to it. It is when he goes to ask his forgiveness that Wilfred is killed, and in his death he gives Max the peace he had lost:

"I'm sorry I struck you, here, the other evening."

"Is that what you came to tell me?" asked Max, laughing contemptuously. "You might just as well have kept your regrets to yourself, for all the good they do me—I thought you were going to talk about your sweetheart. Have you had her? . . . What strikes me most about you is that you always look as though you were making eyes at someone. You look like a choir boy, but like a choir boy who has gone wrong and who makes eyes."[10]

Somewhat later, Wilfred realizes that Max hates him but that his hatred is merely the reverse of a silent but meaningful look in his eyes which turns so quick to anger because Wilfred's answer is invariably negative. Max wanted Wilfred ultimately to give in and at the same give up all faith so that he would become like him, desperate and vicious. Because of his refusal, Max is fascinated by the temptation to kill him. Wilfred leaves the room, and finds himself on the landing, "knowing" that Max is lying in wait for him:

> He went down to the ground floor and pressed the switch button. The light once more showed him the staircase in all its unyielding ugliness. The steps, the banisters, the walls spelt reality, an everyday reality that was beyond argument. There was nothing there that the hand could not touch, the eye could not see. The rest did not exist, the rest was nothing but a dream. "The rest—" he thought, fingering his rosary's little cross as it lay in his pocket. Such thoughts had never entered his head, but they developed in his mind, like a tune that could not be driven away. "The reality of wood and iron, the reality of brick walls, the reality of three steps forward and into the street, the reality of a revolver bullet."
>   . . . [he] peeped out cautiously. . . . He felt that all those windows looked at him with unutterable indifference. At that moment light sprang up around him and he heard Max's soft, precise voice from the second floor landing:
>   "If you move, I'll shoot."
>   The voice seemed to strike at the back of his neck. For a few seconds he remained perfectly still, holding his breath. "I'm going to die," he thought. The idea of praying did not even occur to him, although he had always imagined that certain prayers would come back to him, when he came to

die. What rose within him, as if from the depths of an abyss, was an immense desire to live. . . .

"Close the door and turn round."

"All right," said Wilfred.

He kicked the door open with his foot and bounded forward. The shot went off. Wilfred fell on his face without a sound.

He was curled up on the sidewalk in the attitude of a sleeping child, but he was moaning softly. On his knees by him, Max cried:

"Why did you come here tonight? Say something! Say just anything!"

Bending double suddenly, he brought his lips to Wilfred's ear:

"Say you forgive me," he begged. "Don't go without saying you forgive me! Just say yes. Say yes for the love of Christ!"

Then, with a terrible effort, Wilfred's glance turned slowly towards the murderer, but his eyes rolled back almost immediately. One word was uttered, however, a word that wiped everything away, that redeemed everything because it expressed the greatest love of all. So faintly that Max could scarcely hear, his lips murmured:

"Yes—"

At that moment Wilfred lost consciousness and two policemen ran up from opposite directions.[11]

After Wilfred has been anointed, James Knight, whose wife Wilfred had loved, looks at him and has the following experience of life in death, of a life that is stronger than death:

"When I found myself in that little room again I had to catch hold of the bed's metal bars with both hands, to make sure of standing up straight. I've lived a long time. Never yet have I seen such an expression of happiness on any human face as that which lit up Wilfred's. Applied to him, the word death had no meaning. He was alive, he lived! For a minute I stood plunged in a sort of amazement, then heard myself ask the priest: 'Is it over?' He answered: 'Yes, it is over if you mean that the heart has stopped beating.' I don't know what I said. It is of no importance. I could not keep my eyes from Wilfred. It seemed as though he smiled at my surprise and that he knew secrets and was keeping them to himself. As though he had played a trick on us by going, a boy's prank, and that he was watching us from afar, from a region of light, in spite of the fact that his eyelids were shut. I came closer to him and kissed him twice, three times. I felt a little embarrassed on account of the priest who had dropped on his knees. I think that if I had been alone with Wilfred, I would have talked to him, I would have talked to him for you, if I had known what I know now, I would have talked to him for myself, and for Phoebe too, because he was there, Angus, he was far away and he was near, very near—"[12]

Thus in Julian Green's universe, the operation of grace is bound up with an encounter with others; faith is a light that is illuminated by another light. Grace is made to be communicated; we become aware of it precisely when we do not seek to keep it for ourselves. On the other hand there are several zones of depth in a human being. Grace can act profoundly to aid what we are doing and lead us further than we intended to go. In other words, there are things we do every day: some are good, others bad or indifferent. But at times there are those acts of love of God or neighbor that we do, in which we are impelled by a kind of irresistible call, and which lead us to a point that we had not intended. This is what progressively leads a human being to his salvation. We discover grace to the extent that we do not want to possess it for ourselves and that we agree to its acting in us for others.

*   *   *

In Bernanos' *Diary of a Country Priest*, the Countess admits that she has not forgiven God for taking her son.

"It seems quite plain to me," she said in a voice miraculously different, yet very calm. "Do you know what I was
thinking just now, a moment ago? Perhaps I oughtn't to
tell you what I was thinking. Well, I said to myself: Suppose that in this world or the next, somewhere was a place
where God doesn't exist: though I had to die a thousand
deaths there, to die stoically, every second—well, if it
existed, I'd take my boy to that place" (she dared not call
her dead child by his name) "and I'd say to God: 'Now,
stamp us out! Now do your worst!' I suppose that sounds
horrible to you?"

"No, madame."

"No? How do you mean?"

"Because I too, madame, sometimes I—" I could find no
more words. I could see Dr. Delbende there before me: his
old, tired, inflexible eyes were set on mine, eyes I feared to
read. And I heard, or thought I heard, the groaning of so
many men, their dry sobs, their sighs, the rattle of their
grief, grief of our wretched humanity pressed to earth, its
fearsome murmurings.

"Listen," she said gently, "how can one possibly—? Even
children, even good little children whose hearts are true. . . .
Have you ever seen a child die?"

"No, madame."

"He was so good all the time he was dying. He folded
his little hands, he looked so serious and—and I tried to
make him drink just before it happened—and a drop of
milk was left on his mouth." She was trembling now. I
seemed to be standing there alone between God and this
tortured human being. It was like a huge throbbing in my
breast, but our Lord gave me strength to face her.[13]

We are reminded of the Arab boy, killed in an accident, that
produced Camus's reaction to his friend, saying that heaven
doesn't answer prayers. It also makes us think of the death of
the child of the judge Othon in *The Plague*, when Dr. Rieux
says to Father Paneloux: "You know very well that he was

innocent." To this little child, to these thousands of beloved beings whom death has snatched away from their loved ones; to this mankind marked by fear, a fear that had had Bernanos in its grip from his adolescence, to this humanity "in a winepress"; to all of this, the poor country priest, and thousands of country priests, must bring salvation:

> "Madame," I said, "if our God were a pagan god or the god of intellectuals—and for me it comes to much the same—He might fly to His remotest heaven and our grief would force Him down to earth again. But you know that our God came to be among us. Shake your fist at Him, spit in His face, scourge Him, and finally crucify Him: what does it matter? *My daughter, it's already been done to Him.*" She dared not look at the medallion, which she still held. But how little I realized what she would do.
> "Repeat what you said just now about hell. Hell is—not to love any more."
> "Yes, madame."
> "Well, say it again!"
> "Hell is not to love any more. As long as we remain in this life we can still deceive ourselves, think that we love by our own will, that we love independently of God. But we're like madmen stretching our hands to clasp the moon reflected in water. I'm sorry: I express it so clumsily!"[14]

The priest forces her to repeat with him: "Thy kingdom come; thy will be done," and then the Countess admits:

> "Yes, to you. I've sinned against God. I must have hated Him. Yes, I know now that I should have died with this hate still in my heart, but I won't surrender—except to you."
> "I'm too stupid and insignificant. It's as though you were to put a gold coin in a pierced hand."
> "An hour ago my life seemed so perfectly arranged, everything in its proper place. And you've left nothing standing—nothing at all."[15]

Then, suddenly, as if to indicate that she agrees to commend herself to God, she throws the locket with her child's hair into the fire. The priest dashes to rescue the pathetic memento of the dead child:

> "What madness," I stammered, "how could you dare?"
>
> She had retreated to the wall against which she leaned, and pressed her hands. "I'm sorry." Her voice was humble.
>
> "Do you take God for an executioner? God wants us to be merciful with ourselves. And besides, our sorrows are not our own. He takes them on Himself, into His heart. We have no right to seek them there, mock them, outrage them. Do you understand?"
>
> "What's done is done. I can't help it now."
>
> "My daughter, you must be at peace," I said. And then I blessed her.
>
> My fingers were beginning to bleed a little, the skin had blistered. She tore up a handkerchief and bandaged them. We exchanged no words. The peace I had invoked for her had descended also upon me; and it was so ordinary, so simple, that no outsider could ever have shaken it. For indeed we had returned so quietly to everyday life, that not the most attentive onlooker could have gauged the mystery of this secret, which already was no longer ours.[16]

Quite suddenly, and even with an exaggerated gesture that God did not demand, but which by its significance was the only gesture that could have freed her from her hatred, the Countess accepted her son's death. The priest's mediation, by his words and his presence, overturned her whole life. Nothing was left in place, for truth first enlightens, and then consoles.

A few days later, after the Countess' death, the priest writes in his diary:

> How could I have known that such a day would have no to-morrow, that she and I had faced each other on the very verge of the visible world, over the gulf of All Light? Why could we not have crossed together? "Be at peace," I told her. And she had knelt to receive this peace. May she keep

it for ever. It will be I that gave it her. Oh, miracle—thus
to be able to give what we ourselves do not possess, sweet
miracle of our empty hands! Hope which was shrivelling
in my heart flowered again in hers; the spirit of prayer which
I thought lost in me for ever was given back to her by God
and—who can tell—perhaps in my name! Lord, I am
stripped bare of all things, as you alone can strip us bare,
whose fearful care nothing escapes, nor your terrible love![17]

The priest showed no horror at the Countess' avowal, since
he had also experienced the same risk of despair. It is because
he remained faithful despite everything that he loved others in
everything and that he was able to give the gift he did not
himself possess. Because he did not ask for peace for himself he
was able restore it to the Countess. This is the mystery of the
Communion of Saints. To the extent that we try to be trans-
parent to grace for others, we are ourselves saved. God acts in
the depth of our souls, but by using our own frame of mind and
our own concrete situation. Thus, we are in contact with other
beings who call out to us and we are not always successful in
ignoring their call.

Nevertheless, the Countess' daughter, Chantal, felt that her
mother did not love her, for she preferred her son: she never forgave God. She became resigned, bitter, and full of resentment.
The peace she saw on her mother's face, after the priest's visit,
did more to increase her hatred. Chantal wanted to leave the
house and kill herself. She had a letter in her pocket which was
to announce it to her parents. She went then to see the priest.
She is drawn by him but does not quite know why. She speaks
to him but without telling him what she really wants to do.
During the course of the conversation, the priest asks her for the
letter, the letter she has in her pocket which is so important, in
which she writes about her suicide. Astounded, she answers:
"You're the devil!" But she gives him the letter. She considers
the priest's secret, which attracts her and at the same time pro-
vokes her hatred. Finally the priest answers that she will discover the secret when she has lost it. She will discover the secret
of peace when she has given up peace *for herself* and agreed to
have it only for others.

"Well, I want everything, good and bad, I intend to know everything."

I began to laugh. "You'll soon manage that," I said.

"Not at all. I may be only a girl, but I know quite well that lots of people die before they manage to find out anything."

"Because they were not really looking. They were only dreaming. You'll never dream. The people you mean go round in circles. When you go straight ahead, the world is small."

"What do I care if life lets me down. I'll get my own back. I'll just do evil out of spite!"

"And when you do," I said, "you'll discover God. Oh, no doubt I'm putting it very clumsily. And besides, you're no more than a child. But at least I can tell you this: you are setting off with your back turned on the world, for the world does not stand for revolt, but for submission, submission to lies, first and foremost. Go ahead for all you're worth, the walls are bound to fall in the end, and every breach shows a patch of sky."

"Are you saying all this for the sake of talking—or are you—"

"It is true the meek shall inherit the earth. And your sort won't try and get it from them, because they wouldn't know what to do with it. Snatchers can only snatch at heaven."

She was blushing deeply, and shrugged her shoulders.

"You make me feel I could say anything . . . I'd like to insult you. I won't be disposed of against my will. I'll get to hell all right, if I want to."

"I'll answer for your soul with mine," I said impulsively.

She washed her hands under the kitchen tap, without so much as looking round. Then she quietly put on her hat, which she had taken off when she started working. She came slowly back to me. If I did not know her face so well,

I might have said it looked tranquil, but the corners of her mouth trembled a little.

"I'll make a bargain with you," she said, "if you're what I think you are."

"The point is I am not what you think me. You see yourself in me, as you might in a mirror, and your fate as well."

"When you talked to mother I was hiding under the window. And suddenly her face became so—so gentle. I hated you then. I don't believe much in miracles, not any more than I do in ghosts, but I did think I knew my mother. She cared no more about pretty speeches than a fish for an apple. Have you a secret, yes or no?"

"It's a lost secret," I replied. "You'll rediscover it, and lose it again, and others after you will pass it on, since your kind will last as long as the world."

"My kind? Whatever do you mean?"

"Those whom God sends on and on for ever, who will never rest while the world remains."[18]

For Bernanos, man is not a wise and sensitive "animal" who can deceive himself and choose evil, thinking that his choice was good. This proportioning of instinctive forces is the most total error according to him. In *Under the Sun of Satan*, the pastor of Lumbres had said that evil is loved for itself. As Dostoyevsky had already seen, nothingness is chosen, and sought after, and Bernanos agrees with him. Salvation therefore is not a restful undertaking, but a struggle, a combat, a risk of one's whole self. "It is no laughing matter that I have loved you," Jesus had said to Catherine of Sienna. The unforgettable words that conclude *The Diary of a Country Priest*, "all is grace," do not mean that ultimately the optimists are right, but that crimes and blasphemies are sometimes the road to God, for God came to save what was lost.

The universe of Julian Green, Graham Green and Bernanos is rather abstruse for contemporary men. To perceive the kind of universal truth present in it, we must be in the interior of the domain of the spirit. In the reviews given by non-believers to the works of Mauriac and Julian Green, there is admiration for their psychological force and their style, but they overlook the spiritual drama which is included in the stories themselves and without which they lose all solidity and meaning.

NOTES TO CHAPTER 6

1. A. Blanchet, *La Littérature et le Spirituel*, II (Paris: Aubier, 1960), pp. 136–137.

2. *Dieu-Vivant*, no. 17, 1950, p. 152.

3. Graham Greene, *The Heart of the Matter* (New York: Viking, 1948), p. 306.

4. François Mauriac, *Vipers' Tangle*, trans. Warre B. Wells (New York: Sheed & Ward, 1947), pp. 152–153.

5. *Ibid.*, pp. 250–251.

6. *Ibid.*, pp. 255–256.

7. *Ibid.*, pp. 274–275.

8. *Ibid.*, p. 7.

9. Julian Green, *Each in His Darkness*, trans. by Anne Green (New York: Pantheon, 1961), pp. 69–70.

10. *Ibid.*, pp. 329–330.

11. *Ibid.*, pp. 336–339.

12. *Ibid.*, pp. 346–347.

13. Georges Bernanos, *The Diary of a Country Priest*, trans. Pamela Morris (New York: Macmillan, 1937), pp. 170–171.

14. *Ibid.*, p. 171.

15. *Ibid.*, p. 172.

16. *Ibid.*, pp. 173–174.

17. *Ibid.*, p. 180.

18. *Ibid.*, pp. 254–256.

7

Salvation of the Universe

ONE SECTION OF CHRISTIAN LITERATURE TAKES UP THE THEME OF
salvation as a love that is personal (with T. S. Eliot) or trans-
figuring (Sigrid Undset), or in the light of the resurrection of
human experience in God (Charles Peguy) or, finally, in the
hope of the unity of the Kingdom of God (Paul Claudel, Gertrud von Le Fort).

I. LOVE

1. T. S. ELIOT AND LOVE AS COMMUNION AND PARDON

The Anglo-American poet, T. S. Eliot, is possibly best known
for his play *Murder in the Cathedral*. It is a lyrical and at times
liturgical account of the martyrdom of Thomas à Becket, Archbishop of Canterbury, on December 29, 1170. If we read Jean
Anouilh's *Becket*, we see the great gulf that separates the two
works. Anouilh's play tells us much about its author but nothing
about Becket or the honor of God. On the contrary, with Eliot,
the death of the martyred bishop is kind of leaven of the unity
willed by God for his Church and his people.

Before his conversion to Anglicanism, Eliot was haunted by
the emptiness of human life. He expresses this obsession in his
famous poem *The Hollow Men*:

>   We are the hollow men
>   We are the stuffed men
>   Leaning together

Headpiece filled with straw. Alas!
Our dried voices, when
We whisper together
Are quiet and meaningless
As wind in dry grass
Or rats' feet over broken glass
In our dry cellar

Shape without form, shade without colour,
Paralysed force, gesture without motion;

Those who have crossed
With direct eyes, to death's other Kindgom
Remember us—if at all—not as lost
Violent souls, but only
As the hollow men
The stuffed men.[1]

This disquiet, mingled with despair, is expressed by the chorus of Canterbury women at the beginning of *Murder in the Cathedral*:

Some malady is coming upon us. We wait, we wait,
And the saints and martyrs wait, for those who shall be martyrs and saints.
Destiny waits in the hand of God, shaping the still unshapen:
I have seen these things in a shaft of sunlight.
Destiny waits in the hand of God, not in the hands of statesmen
Who do, some well, some ill, planning and guessing,
Having their aims which turn in their hands in the pattern of time.
Come, happy December, who shall observe you, who shall preserve you?
Shall the Son of Man be born again in the litter of scorn?
For us, the poor, there is no action,
But only to wait and to witness.[2]

From one text to the other, within the same disquiet, there
is the transition from the anguish of emptiness in a world of
"shape without form," to resigned expectation which is under-
lined by a thread of hope.

The summit of the drama is at the moment that Thomas
Becket chooses God rather than men. It is because of this that
the King is driving him to the wall. If he gives in to the royal
blackmail, the sovereign power of the Word of God would be
absent, and it alone is capable of making free men out of these
colorless shades that we are, whether kings or churls. One part
of the Archbishop's monologue illustrates this point of intense
abandonment to a crucifying salvation:

> Now is my way clear, now is the meaning plain:
> Temptation shall not come in this kind again.
> The last temptation is the greatest treason:
> To do the right deed for the wrong reason.
>
> . . . .
>
> While I ate out of the King's dish
> To become servant of God was never my wish.
> Servant of God has chance of greater sin
> And sorrow than the man who serves a king.
>
> . . . .
>
>   I know
> What yet remains to show you of my history
> Will seem to most of you at best futility,
> Senseless self-slaughter of a lunatic,
> Arrogant passion of a fanatic.
> I know that history at all times draws
> The strangest consequence from remotest cause.
> But for every evil, every sacrilege,
> Crime, wrong, oppression and the axe's edge,
> Indifference, exploitation, you, and you,
> And you, must all be punished. So must you.
> I shall no longer act or suffer, to the sword's end.
> Now my good Angel, whom God appoints
> To be my guardian, hover over the swords' points.[3]

The sermon pronounced by Thomas Becket in his cathedral
on Christmas morning, 1170, is one of the most beautiful pages
I know. One passage will allow us a glimpse of the spiritual
ascension of a believer:

> . . . For whenever Mass is said, we re-enact the Passion
> and death of Our Lord; and on this Christmas Day we do
> this in celebration of His Birth . . . so it is only in these
> our Christian mysteries that we can rejoice and mourn at
> once for the same reason. But think for a while on the
> meaning of this word 'peace.' Does it seem strange to you
> that the angels should have announced Peace, when cease-
> lessly the world has been stricken with War and the fear of
> War? Does it seem to you that the angelic voices were
> mistaken, and that the promise was a disappointment and
> a cheat?
>
> Reflect now, how Our Lord Himself spoke of Peace. . . .
> What then did he mean? If you ask that, remember then
> that He said also, 'Not as the world gives, give I unto you.'
> So then, He gave to His disciples peace, but not peace as
> the world gives.
>
> . . . A martyr, a saint, is always made by the design of God,
> for His love of men, to warn them and to lead them, to
> bring them back to His ways. A martyrdom is never the
> design of man; for the true martyr is he who has become
> the instrument of God, who has lost his will in the will of
> God, not lost it but found it, for he has found freedom in
> submission to God. . . .
>
> I have spoken to you today, dear children of God, of the
> martyrs of the past, asking you to remember especially our
> martyr of Canterbury, the blessed Archbishop Elphege;
> because it is fitting, on Christ's birth day, to remember what
> is that Peace which He brought; and because, dear chil-
> dren, I do not think I shall ever preach to you again; and
> because it is possible that in a short time you may have yet
> another martyr, and that one perhaps not the last. I would

have you keep in your hearts these words that I say, and think of them at another time. In the Name of the Father and of the Son, and of the Holy Ghost. Amen.[4]

After the assassination of the Archbishop, the final chorus expresses the Christian faith and hope that he had begun to see and accept:

Forgive us, O Lord, we acknowledge ourselves as type of
   the common man,
Of the men and women who shut the door and sit by the
   fire;
Who fear the blessing of God, the loneliness of the night
   of God, the surrender required, the deprivation inflicted;
Who fear the injustice of men less than the justice of God;
Who fear the hand at the window, the fire in the thatch,
   the fist in the tavern, the push into the canal,
Less than we fear the love of God.
We acknowledge our trespass, our weakness, our fault; we
   acknowledge
That the sin of the world is upon our heads; that the blood
   of the martyrs and the agony of the saints
Is upon our heads.
Lord, have mercy upon us.
Christ, have mercy upon us.
Lord, have mercy upon us.
Blessed Thomas, pray for us.[5]

These last words, borrowed from the liturgy, show that the confession of sin, the call to salvation and hope in God are not an abstract discovery, but a concrete event, originating in the Archbishop's martyrdom. The giving of his life for his people begins to work the ingathering of this ordinary people that fears the blessing of God, begins to gather it together in the hope of salvation.

*   *   *

This work, so deeply influenced by medieval mystery plays, is a sort of lyrical testimony—in a style in which nobility and sensitivity are intermingled—to the faith in salvation, beyond hatred. Eliot's other writings increasingly abandon the explicitly tragic form and turn to a theater of daily life, where all we see are the trivial intrigues of worldly people, although the author has very profoundly interwoven into the fabric some of the great Greek myths, Alcestis, Orpheus, Ion, Oedipus at Colonus. Beyond this second level of "illumination"—to use Gabriel Marcel's word—there is a third level, that of Christian salvation, where we pass from the shadow of love to the hope of communion.

Eliot has given an explanation about the aim of his poetic dramas. He believes poetry is the normal form of serious drama. This form unconsciously extends the spectators' experience and makes them perceive a deeper dimension to their daily existence, one which their ordinary consciousness does not perceive. In other words, by giving expression to the character of the men pronouncing them, the words also express something other than the character in the ordinary sense of the word. For a few seconds life is raised to the dignity of the dance or the liturgy, with an ardor that is found in all great poetry and a much deeper seriousness beneath the ardor. In fact, it is the privilege of dramatic poetry to be able to show us several levels of reality all at once.

Undoubtedly Eliot's thoughts refer specifically to Shakespeare, but his own dramatic work is written in the same line. Particularly in *The Cocktail Party* the "mundane" encounter of the characters is completely drenched with a deeper presence—to be more more precise, the presence of salvation. Without any seeming change in the unfolding of the most banal and mundane encounter, we first have a presentiment of a more essential dimension, which is perceived and ultimately the subject of contemplation. Without any break we pass from the level of daily reality to the plane of hell and loneliness, ultimately to progress along the road of faith. In fact, it is even wrong to speak of successive planes or levels. The same reality becomes deeply illuminated and unveils stages of meaning. A kind of liturgy of people in search of salvation appears. The hope for salvation, however, never appears as a *deus ex machina*. Here, in a profoundly English context, we have a kind of Platonism diffused into the sensible, which Gabriel Marcel calls "illumination."

With merely a few quotations it is no easy matter to give the

sense of this discovery of the road of salvation that these characters have all made. Eliot is perhaps the writer who has been
best able to intertwine the absence and the presence of divine
hope in the tissue of daily life, the life that men call "real."

After *Murder in the Cathedral*, and through *The Family
Reunion*, which seems to be a transitional play, we see that the
author no longer has a need for referring explicitly to the leg-
ends and myths of antiquity. The *Eumenides* of *The Family
Reunion* have disappeared in *The Cocktail Party*. These works
have been called "pocket" tragedies. Perhaps. In any case, they
take place in a drawing room. The characters come together for
cocktails. The conversation is merely gossip, a type of conversation used to avoid too many silences and to keep people from
saying what they think. Edward has just been left by his wife
Lavinia. He is discovering that basically he did not love Celia,
his mistress. She loved him but with a stubborn feeling of being
unsatisfied, for the half-seen treasure unceasingly escaped her.
An unknown guest speaks to Edward and we guess that Edward
does not yet know anything about him. Another character,
particularly in the first act, appears to be a buffoon: Julia, a
kind of English old maid, keeps leaving the apartment and
coming back, forgetting her umbrella or her glasses (which she
discovers in her purse). In reality, this apparent bore has perceived the drama that is underway with Edward, Celia, and
Lavinia. Impelled by a sort of divination, she wants to prevent
the irreparable.

Who *is* this person? A messenger? Someone sent from God?
But Julia has never heard a voice that would have made any
impression. She is too involved in everyday existence. Yet she
is God's messenger, and her coming a kind of Advent, for she is
preparing the way. But at no moment does "the sky open" or
does a "ray from heaven" come down. It is at the core of the
simplest of situations that the significance, the most secret
sense of a life, is disclosed. She is thus preparing the way for
the unknown guest. In the second act he is revealed as a neurol-
ogist, but through his cures, he will truly appear as a lover of
men (*philanthropos*) and one who places them on the road
to salvation.

Edward soon discovers that his life is a hell:

> There was a door.
> And I could not open it. I could not touch the handle.
> Why could I not walk out of my prison?
> What is hell? Hell is oneself,
> Hell is alone, the other figures in it
> Merely projections. There is nothing to escape from
> And nothing to escape to. One is always alone. . . .
> I am simply in hell. Where there are no doctors—
> At least, not in a professional capacity.[6]

This theme that the others and we ourselves are "shadow men" when we are exiled from our true reality is central with Eliot. He is related both to Shakespearian and Platonic themes, but he also brings out, in this play especially, the shadowy road that leads to the kingdom of the dead from which Heracles rescued Alcestis and Orpheus, Eurydice.

Hell is isolation. Only, here we find ourselves in the presence of an impossibility of loving that is much more radical than one resulting uniquely from a psychological error, an absence of sexual harmony, or intellectual or moral disparity. We are dealing with a *fundamental* impossibility of passing from shadow to reality, of emerging from inveterate selfishness.

Doctor Reilly, the mysterious guest of the first act, who receives Edward in his medical office, explains this to him: he tells Edward that he was never truly in love with Celia and that in fact he has never been in love with anyone, which made him suspect that he was incapable of loving at all. And he has now come to discover that no one had ever loved him. Then, Dr. Reilly concludes, he began to fear that no one *could* love him. Celia soon discovers that she too has taken the wrong road:

> No . . . it isn't that I *want* to be alone
> But that everyone's alone—or so it seems to me.
> They make noises, and think they are talking to each other;
> They make faces, and think they understand each other.
> And I'm sure that they don't. Is that a delusion?[7]

Even in her adulterous love for Edward, she discovers failure:

Oh, I thought that I was giving him so much!
And he to me—and the giving and the taking
Seemed so right: not in terms of calculation
Of what was good for the persons we had been
But for the new person, us. If I could feel
As I did then, even now it would seem right.
And then I found we were only strangers
And that there had been neither giving nor taking
But that we had merely made use of each other
Each for his purpose. That's horrible. Can we only love
Something created by our own imagination?
Are we all in fact unloving and unlovable?
Then one is alone, and if one is alone
Then lover and beloved are equally unreal
And the dreamer is no more real than his dreams.[8]

We see that disclosure deprives the *exile* in which we all live of all its trappings. It makes us feel a captivity from which there is no way out. Edward, Lavinia, and Peter have lived within an image that was fashioned to their own needs.

The meaning of this exile, however, becomes illuminated a bit when it appears connected with a fault, intermingled with guilt. This Celia discovers at the same time as her radical loneliness. Here we are dealing with a guilt experience that goes far deeper than "ordinary immorality."

. . . But first I must tell you
That I should really *like* to think there's something wrong
    with me—
Because, if there isn't, then there's something wrong,
Or at least, very different from what it seemed to be,
With the world itself—and that's much more frightening!
That would be terrible. So I'd rather believe
There is something wrong with me. . . .[9]

We will recall that Kafka had already told us that in a combat between the world and the self, it is the world that must be upheld. In fact, Kafka always refused to accuse the world and declare it absurd; he preferred to accuse himself. Instead of these characters proclaiming their innocence in the face of a world bereft of meaning, they know they are guilty and "law-less." Moreover, we have pointed out the importance in its time of this "Copernican revolution" that came about in Kafka's moral universe. We have seen in it a stepping-stone to salvation, explicitly absent from the universe of Sartre or Simone de Beauvoir. It is all the more significant to find this same notation made again in *The Cocktail Party*, but this time it is at the beginning of an itinerary that will lead to the discovery of salvation.

Yet, this guilt is so radical that it is situated beyond any ordinary action that might be forgotten or disavowed. It is most profoundly rooted in life itself, and thus reaches a fundamental situation, an "existential."

> It's not the feeling of anything I've ever done,
> Which I might get away from, or of anything in me
> I could get rid of—but of emptiness, of failure
> Towards someone, or something, outside of myself;
> And I feel I must . . . atone—is that the word?
> Can you treat a patient for such a state of mind?[10]

Dr. Reilly, who at times makes us think of the "psychological" angels, or the angel that appeared to Tobias, knows that there is salvation. It is close at hand and far away at the same time. But the first and indispensable step is to begin by acknowledging that we are incapable of crossing the phantasmagoria of the shadows, and of truly loving others. He tells this to Edward and Lavinia:

> And now you begin to see, I hope,
> How much you have in common. The same isolation.
> A man who finds himself incapable of loving
> And a woman who finds that no man can love her.[11]

Therefore he will tell them to be of good heart against ill fortune. He will soon describe to Celia how these people can remain together in their daily lives, but this time without the false idea that they can truly love one another:

> I can reconcile you to the human condition,
> The condition to which some who have gone as far as you

Have succeeded in returning. They may remember
The vision they have had, but they cease to regret it,
Maintain themselves by the common routine,
Learn to avoid excessive expectation,
Become tolerant of themselves and others,
Giving and taking, in the usual actions
What there is to give and take. They do not repine;
Are contented with the morning that separates
And with the evening that brings together
For casual talk before the fire
Two people who know they do not understand each other,
Breeding children whom they do not understand
And who will never understand them.[12]

Edward and Lavinia will live this life. Yet, knowing that they are but exiles from themselves, "shadows of desires of desires,"[13] they accept what Reilly tells them:

Your business is not to clear your conscience
But to learn how to bear the burdens on your conscience.[14]

We see them together, two years later. They are at peace, since they have accepted the fact that they are not capable of loving one another by themselves. Through this they have found a kind of closeness in the humble acceptance of their limitations:

I like the dress you're wearing:
I'm glad you put on that one.
    LAVINIA: Well, Edward!
Do you know it's the first time you've paid me a compliment
Before a party? And that's when one needs them.[15]

Celia took the "short" road, the one that demands a break, a departure with no return. Actually she did have a vision of something which she could no longer pass up. She can no longer give to anyone this kind of love that belongs to this life. What she had lived with Edward, even in her failure, taught her the existence of a lost treasure. This road Reilly explains to her:

There *is* another way, if you have the courage.
The first I could describe in familiar terms
Because you have seen it, as we all have seen it,
Illustrated, more or less, in lives of those about us.
The second is unknown, and so requires faith—
The kind of faith that issues from despair.
The destination cannot be described;
You will know very little;
You will journey blind. But the way leads towards posses-
    sion
Of what you have sought for in the wrong place. . . .
No lonelier than the other. But those who take the other
Can forget their loneliness. You will not forget yours.
Each way means loneliness—and communion.
Both ways avoid the final desolation
Of solitude in the phantasmal world
Of imagination, shuffling memories and desires.[16]

The only worthwhile adventure is the passage from shadow to
reality, from the illusion of the unsubstantial likeness to the
archetypal truth. This world of representation, where others are
too often merely the echo of our desires and our hatreds and
constantly elude us, is hell begun on earth. The true world can
be glimpsed once we begin by accepting loneliness which is also
communion, for it respects the truth of the other, the other's
inaccessibility and our own inability to get through the clouds
of the phantasmagoria.

Along this "path," this "roadway," there are no signposts, no
welcoming inns, no lights outside of ourselves. For it we need
that kind of faith that springs from despair: we know nothing of
our destination before reaching it. How can we not think of that
mystery spoken of by Gabriel Marcel? How can this not remind
us, and this time explicitly, of Orpheus' voyage when he sought
Eurydice on the way of the dead and could be with her only
if he refused to look at her, question her, assure himself about
her presence, and unceasingly supervise her? This "mystery" is
thus a reality which does not become illuminated of itself. One
can never sit down and examine it to be sure that it gives light.
The "mystery" is an obscure reality, which still lights up the

way: if we look at the light of the torch we are blinded and see nothing, but if we agree to go on our way carrying the torch, the way is lighted before us:

> There is certainly no purpose in remaining in the dark
> Except long enough to clear from the mind
> The illusion of having ever been in the light.[17]

Therefore, this road that crosses the "dark night" recalls the journeys of the Greeks beyond the grave. On the golden tablets one read: "Keep to the right toward the meadows of Prosephone." But it also reminds us of the voyage of Tobias and the road to Carmel, through the "living flame of love." For it we need guardian presences and secret protectors, we need the invocation for travellers:

> Protector of travellers
> Bless the road
>> ALEX:
> Watch over her in the desert
> Watch over her in the mountain
> Watch over her in the labyrinth
> Watch over her by the quicksand.
>> JULIA:
> Protect her from the Voices
> Protect her from the Visions
> Protect her in the tumult
> Protect her in the silence.[18]

Along this route, where our steps awaken echoes of the labyrinth of antiquity, the Minotaur's lair, where bats gave out their tiny plaintive cries, we need messengers to direct our way so that we never lose our Eurydice, precisely because we have agreed not to look at her.

Celia leaves for India. She lives with lepers and the poor. Her lot is with the dying Indians, condemned to death through the inevitable plague. She is crucified near these corpses by a neighboring tribe. But this "useless" death, this "futile" love, living with the dying to give them at least a last small taste of life, the sign that they too, and especially they, are loved, will illuminate those who have stayed "at home": Edward and Lavinia, and Peter who finally understands the meaning of his love for Celia. During the cocktail party Reilly had seen

> . . . the image, standing behind her chair,
> Of a Celia Coplestone whose face showed the astonishment
> Of the first five minutes after a violent death. . . .
>   So all that I could do
> Was to direct her in the way of preparation.[19]

Reilly can therefore bring the decisive light into the lives of those who have remained this side of the veil. He says to Edward and Lavinia:

> You will have to live with these memories and make them
> Into something new. Only by acceptance
> Of the past will you alter its meaning.[20]

It is quite wonderful to see a subtle correspondence between works that a world separates. In *Hiroshima mon amour*, the young Frenchwoman would not accept the fact that the delicious and guilty loves of her adolescence in Nevers were dead. At times she forgot them, at times recalled them, as one recalls the dead in a kind of paralyzing nirvana, which fascinated her and fixed her in a "nowhere" of time and space, making her life into a nightmare. What she should have done was to accept the past, to accept its reality, that it *was* and that it is no more. Only then could she have discovered the meaning of the death of her love. By accepting the past, Edward and Lavinia give it meaning. They will live out Paul Ricoeur's worthy remark: "Hope is the same as reminiscence." Reminiscence. Not the magic remembrance that resurrects a vanished past in a kind of wake dream, nor the withering of a person living out a dead love of the past, nor the meanderings of an interior Lethe with its six-fold windings. But an open and confident memory, searching for a future made up of the acceptance of the past. A memory enlightened from within by a clarity from behind and "from on high" which softly lights up the cavern of this world and prepares us for the true light.

The marvel in Eliot's work is that the ongoing path of salvation is foretold through mundanity. Nothing is explicitly assert-

ed. The name of Christ or God is never uttered. Undoubtedly
there is a recurring refrain: "Work out your salvation with dili-
gence,"[21] inspired by Philippians 2:12: "Work out your own
salvation with fear and trembling." Through this allusion we
have a glimpse of the author's Christianity. But this is only a
more obvious trace in a page where, as we have said, we uncover
the great religious myths of the path to salvation.

Thus, starting with the "closed" universe of non-believing
writers, and going beyond St.-John Perse who focussed on man
and his renewal, we make our way toward the light of salvation.
In the chiaroscuro of Eliot's work, where phantoms mingle
with the living, where humor brings these "dream-people" alive,
where there is a crisscross of Platonic voyages in the core of
sensitive love, "the way, the truth and the life," we see forming
the beginnings of a love-communion between the living and the
dead. Salvation-in-love becomes identified with the phrase from
the Gospels: "No greater love has any man than that he lay
down his life for those he loves."

*   *   *

I have just mentioned the closed universe of our non-believing friends. In my opinion, as Henry Fluchère said in his French
translation of the play (1959), *The Elder Statesman* is probably
the most anti-Sartrian play Eliot has written. Fluchère makes a
particular contrast with Sartre's *No Exit*. For my part, I should
like to show how this play is a kind of "before-the-fact" response
to the drama of Franz von Gerlach in *The Condemned of
Altona*. The echoes and responses found inscribed in the very
fabric of this work seem more enlightening than explicit com-
mentary.

Henry Fluchère, to whom I owe my essential knowledge of
Eliot, underlines very remarkably how the Oedipus myth is here
constantly underlying. In *The Condemned of Altona*, the father
knows that he is guilty in regard to Franz. In *The Elder Statesman*, Lord Claverton also discovers that he has never really been
a father to his son Michael. The son says to him:

What is my inheritance? . . .
I was just *your* son—that is to say,
A kind of prolongation of your existence,

A representative carrying on business in your absence.
Why should I thank you for imposing this on me?[22]

Like Franz, who knows the injustices committed by his
father, Michael wonders aloud whether his father observed the
law:

. . . Those standards of conduct
You've always made so much of, for my benefit:
I wonder whether you have always lived up to them.[23]

More and more clearly Lord Claverton knows that his life is
based on a series of bad actions committed in his youth. The
kind of family reunion assembled about him, in the small hotel
where he is staying, consists of a school friend from Oxford,
Gomez, and a woman to whom he promised marriage and
whom he then abandoned, since she would have been harmful
to his career. It is more of an appearance than a reunion.
Through these characters, it is the voice of his conscience that
speaks to him. One evening as a young student he was coming
home with Gomez and two frivolous girls, and he ran over an
old man with his car. The old man was already dead, but they
did not know it. They did not stop. Gomez was fascinated by
the young Claverton, to the point of having his soul touched,
but he was also incapable of ever extricating himself from his
spell. The future peer had promised to marry a young woman.
He had even possessed her and then left her after buying back
his promise of marriage. Such a union with a girl who at the
time was an unknown (later she became a music-hall entertainer)
would have impeded his political and financial career. With his
wife he lived constantly as one alone, never really daring to cross
the desert separating them. As for his son, as we have mentioned, he merely turned him into an extension of himself. Of
him might be said what the father said to Franz in *The Condemned of Altona:* "Your future was made only with my past."

So, Lord Claverton is an honorable man who has built his life
upon the absence of love. He contemplates nothingness and is
always alone. He has become the elder statesman, in golden
retirement, and with a peerage.

Lord Claverton is also a man who has questions about his
past. What Eliot insinuates is the image of Oedipus. Oedipus,

who killed his father and married his mother, who at the beginning of *Oedipus Rex* orders passionately and imperiously that a search be made for the guilty person whose crime has blackened the city of Thebes. The culprit is himself, Oedipus the King; it is Claverton the peer.

However, at the end of his wanderings during which he exiled himself from the face of the living, Oedipus arrives near Athens at the town of Colonus, where the olive trees whisper, the violets send out their scent, and the nightingales sing. Oedipus is accompanied by his daughter Antigone, who has not left him. Lord Claverton, too, has a daughter, Monica. In his old age, he too has taken refuge in the country in a kind of combination hospital and rest home in which the sick are cared for in surroundings that dissimulate their illnesses and only manifest the pleasant company of distinguished guests. Lord Claverton too has arrived at Colonus. What will save him is that he too has a daughter, an Antigone to hear his confession, who loves and understands him. In this rediscovered filial love she will find a new illumination that will deepen her love for her fiancé, Charles Hemington. The drama of the father in *The Condemned of Altona* is to have a daughter, who is the opposite of an Antigone. Instead of Leni's making an effort to help her brother and to understand her father, she is Franz's accomplice and gives in to her hatred for her father. She returns indifference for indifference, hatred for hatred.

What we need at certain times, more than bread and water, is to be understood and listened to by someone who tries to understand but who at the same time is not an accomplice in our weaknesses, but reveals them and shows them to us, and leads us to a kind of confession where the demand for forgiveness is legibly written. Monica, Lord Claverton's daughter, is an Antigone. She is like that voice of conscience Du Bos speaks of, "the elder brother who goes before us on our way," who never discourages us but also never encourages us when we give in.

The wonder of the play is that even in the father's confession to his daughter there is a kind of peace that spreads progressively through the "most bitter bitterness." We should not look for a "why." Here we have a human mediation which of itself produces alleviation. Nothing seems more contrary to fatherhood than a father's confessing his faults to his daughter. And yet, it is in this very confession that we have drawn a more noble image of fatherhood in which Lord Claverton and Monica share. Because both discover one another and accept one another (even though they were deprived of genuine paternity), they find it and share in it again: Lord Claverton as a father and his daughter in her filial relationship. From the world of shades, we make the transition to the world of reality.

But first we must meet someone who can accept the total secret. This is what Lord Claverton says to Charles:

> If there's nothing, truly nothing, that you couldn't tell
> Monica
> Then all is well with you. You're in love with each other—
> . . . And if there is nothing that you conceal from *her*
> However important you may consider it
> To conceal from the rest of the world—your soul is safe.
> If a man has one person, just one in his life,
> To whom he is willing to confess everything—
> And that includes, mind you, not only things criminal,
> Not only turpitude, meanness and cowardice,
> But also situations which are simply ridiculous,
> When he has played the fool (as who has not?)—
> Then he loves that person, and his love will save him.[24]

Lord Claverton realizes that he has never made such a confidence. He also knows that he cannot be completely honest with his child if has never been with someone older. Nevertheless, he attempts the great adventure of saying to his daughter that he was never the person she thought he was:

> I've had your love under false pretences.
> Now, I'm tired of keeping up those pretences,
> But I hope that you'll find a little love in your heart
> Still, for your father, when you know him
> For what he is, the broken-down actor.[25]

Lord Claverton's daughter is the antithesis of Leni in *The Condemned of Altona*. She answers:

> I think I should only love you the better, Father,
> The more I knew about you. I should understand you
> better.

There's nothing I'm afraid of learning about Charles,
There's nothing I'm afraid of learning about you.[26]

Somewhat earlier she told her father that she would have
given her life for him and added:

Oh, how silly that phrase sounds! But there's no vocabulary
For love within a family, love that's lived in
But not looked at, love within the light of which
All else is seen, the love within which
All other love finds speech.
This love is silent.[27]

Lord Claverton's confession clothes a particularly strong sense
of calm because it is inscribed within a meditation on filial love.
As his daughter says, this love bathes everything we see with
light, even though we do not see the love. Gabriel Marcel has
often said that the "mystery" is a light that illumines the road
if we keep the torch overhead, without wanting to look into
the light, without wanting unceasingly to verify, take measure-
ments, and to have guarantees. Family life is one of these realities. The marvel glimpsed by Sophocles in *Oedipus at Colonus*,
Shakespeare in *King Lear* and Eliot in *The Elder Statesman*, *is*
that in the twilight of his life the father, who discovers his emptiness, the thinness of his unsubstantial shadow, also encounters
another life, young and fresh, which has come from him and
comes to him in dialogue, to listen to him and with him to
discover a "family mystery" in which all share.

When Lord Claverton confesses to his daughter that he has
carried within himself alone the ghost of the dead old man on
the highway, he wonders whether he can ever get absolution:

They are merely ghosts:
Spectres from my past. They've always been with me
                                   . . . and I see myself emerging
From my spectral existence into something like reality.
  MONICA:
But what did the ghosts mean? All these years
You've kept them to yourself. Did Mother know of them?
  LORD CLAVERTON:
Your mother knew nothing about them. And I know

That I never knew your mother, as she never knew me.
I thought that she would never understand
Or that she would be jealous of the ghosts who haunted me.
And I'm still of that opinion. How open one's heart
When one is sure of the wrong response?
How make a confession with no hope of absolution?[28]

It is at this moment that Monica becomes identified with the eternal Antigone in what she says:

It is time to break the silence! Let us share your ghosts!
        CHARLES:
But these are only human beings, who can be dealt with.
        MONICA: Or only ghosts, who can be exorcised![29]

At the end of his admissions we see almost in plain view the mysterious reality which I can only call "mediation" because it is really in the voice and countenance of his daughter that Lord Claverton has a glimpse of that deep peace that follows confession and is the dawn of salvation:

I shan't run away now—run away from *them.*
It is through this meeting that I shall at last escape them.
—I've made my confession to you, Monica:
That is the first step taken towards my freedom,
And perhaps the most important. I know what you think.
You think that I suffer from a morbid conscience,
From brooding over faults I might well have forgotten.
You think that I'm sickening, when I'm just recovering!
It's hard to make other people realise
The magnitude of things that appear to them petty;
It's harder to confess the sin that no one believes in
Than the crime that everyone can appreciate.
For the crime is in relation to the law
And the sin is in relation to the sinner.
What has made the difference in the last five minutes
Is not the heinousness of my misdeeds
But the fact of my confession. And to you, Monica,
To you, of all people.[30]

The fact of the confession is what counts. The hidden and secret sin eats away. It is not a confession to just anyone, but to a person who shares in the mystery of the family, in that relationship of fatherhood-sonship. To break it is the beginning of woe, and to restore it in humility is the way of salvation.

Therefore, Lord Claverton feels in peace, and says so in words that remind us of the conclusion of Oedipus at Colonus:

Why did I always want to dominate my children?
Why did I mark out a narrow path for Michael?
Because I wanted to perpetuate myself in him.
Why did I want to keep you to myself, Monica?
Because I wanted you to give your life to adoring
The man that I pretended to myself that I was,
So that I could believe in my own pretences.
I've only just now had the illumination
Of knowing what love is. We all think we know,
But how few of us do! And now I feel happy—
In spite of everything, in defiance of reason,
I have been brushed by the wing of happiness.
And I am happy, Monica, that you have found a man
Whom you can love for the man he really is.[31]

When Monica answers, the circle is closed again:

Oh Father, I've always loved you,
But I love you more since I have come to know you
Here, at Badgley Court. And I love you the more
Because I love Charles.[32]

A unity is sensed. Something of the mutual communication of father and child is to be seen, descending and ascending, redescending and reascending.

It is quite noticeable that the Christian references are most discreet. Eliot merely hints at the Christian dimension beyond the family reunion, even beyond the Greek myth. And we shall certainly not reproach him for it. In fact, it is in the very heart of human relationship, lived in its totality, that the grace of salvation appears and acts. It ought not be represented as a kind of meteorite falling from heaven, nor, we repeat, as a ray from the clouds that settles on someone's brow. The only thing "pious" about that sort of image is its name! The grace of salvation acts with the help of the psychological mechanism it encounters. It goes about in disguise in the same corridors and drawing rooms where Mrs. Piggott, the gossipy proprietor of the sanitarium-hotel, ranted and raved. It speaks in the voice of a simple girl and also in the lower voice of a statesman confessing the truth of his life.

It is on account of the exemplary discretion of Eliot's work that it merits a special place at the core of this essay. I am mistrustful of religious lessons that are too wordy, cautions that are too vociferous and helping hands that are too ostentatious. The path of God's grace is through "second causes" as Malègue said. The same event can be seen in various depths. The threefold dimension of Eliot's theater, worldly, Greek, and Christian, seems to me to be exceptionally important for our study.

*　　*　　*

The feeling of Eliot's work is very "English." Maurice Baring wrote about his own conversion to Catholicism that it was the only action of his life that he never regretted. In Daphne Adeane he evokes the presence of a young Englishwoman who has died. Only her portrait remains. Yet his theme is quite different from Oscar Wilde's Picture of Dorian Gray, where the portrait itself bore all the marks of the hero's life, fascinated him, and progressively led him into a kind of vertigo of pleasure and damnation. Daphne Adeane's picture, on the contrary, operates progressively as a mediating presence. It is no longer merely a reminder of the dead but a presence that answers the invocation. Actually, the picture inhabits the souls of all who thought they knew Daphne Adeane, who knew her more or less, who are not sure of having really known her. This presence of a dead girl, still close to those who have remained in the world arena, leads the principal characters to an awareness of the real problem facing them, the problem of death and life, of hatred and love.

English literature is very marked by a metaphysical diffusion into the tangible. On the religious and Christian level it gives a glimpse of the presence of a religious reality that is suspended within the most real, banal, and "English" of human societies.

2. SIGRID UNDSET AND TRANSFIGURED LOVE

The Norwegian writer, Sigrid Undset, is no longer so widely read today, and this is a pity. Her work is dominated by the problem of sin and grace, but in a perspective that is more universal than Eliot's. In her first period, prior to her conversion, she writes about modern Norwegian youth, particularly young women. They are unhappy, lost in a materialistic and naturalistic society, deeply marked by the positivism of the 1880's and also by extraordinary social success. They are in quest of a love that is close to vegetable and animal nature. A kind of dream of pagan life inhabits them. But all they find are firstfruits and beginnings.

A novel, *Gymnadenia*, which is composed of two separate works: *The Burning Bush* and *The Wild Orchid*, gives us the story of Paul Selmer. It is sort of Sigrid Undset's *Wilhelm Meister*, since it tells of her hero's years of formation. Paul Selmer has a mother who is filled with the ideas of 1880 positivism. He is a pagan. He met a girl, Lucy, and tries to experience a total love with her, where tenderness and sensuality attempt to rediscover the road to a kind of "naturistic" paradise.

> "Don't be so silly, Lucy," he begged her with a laugh. Then she obediently climbed out of the boat and disappeared among the bushes.
>
> He was undressed in no time. Jolly to get out of one's trousers. He stretched himself and surveyed with approval his brown, well-trained body—admired the play of his muscles as he changed his position to get the full benefit of the caresses of sun and air. It was brown, peaty soil, with some tufts of sedge and here and there cushions of light green moss and of fragile, cool stellaria—he walked a few paces, it was so good to tread on with bare feet.
>
> "Lucy," he called softly. "Come along—shall I give you a hand—"
>
> She came out and stood, dazzlingly golden white, in front of an osier bush which reflected sunshine from all its shiny leaves. She raised one arm above her head—a twig had caught in her hair: the line from the elbow along the

inside of her upper arm, the armpit and one breast which was raised by the movement, the waist and the arch of the hip, the thigh which was lost in the tissue of grass—it was so beautiful that he could have wept! But when he called her name and made as though he would spring at her, she gave vent to little pitiful screams, doubled up and waved him off with her arms—he saw the same agonized blush on her face and far over her neck—

Then he checked himself:

"No but, Lucy—" he tried to laugh. The sun kissed her all over; some belated buttercups bloomed in the grass at her feet—but the girl's incomprehensible fear projected as it were an invisible wall between them. The wild and joyous excitement dropped from him; he felt his heart contract at something strange and meaningless.—Then he turned his back to her, took the few paces down to the water's edge and plunged in.[33]

A wall, invisible and unsurmountable, has grown up between Paul and Lucy, although everything ought to have brought them together: their love of the water, the sun, and their own bodies, a love that is so passionate in the brief Scandinavian summers. This glass wall is a sign of something else: love is much more than love. Mysteriously we are shut off and separated, and nothing is more false than the apparent naturalness of "naturistic" love, an idea still quite current today.

A long time after, a convert to Catholicism and a married man with children, Paul thinks again about this scene and he understands its profound meaning more clearly. Even at that time, since they were brought up in positivism, far away from any explicit faith, Lucy and Paul perceived the presence of something else only because they loved one another. It was the presence of a kind of exile from which human love must be saved by searching for its homeland, a country that we *never* completely discover on earth:

The reasonable explanation is that which calls us the exiled children of Eve. And who could tell whether in his heart he had not been assured that the latter explanation was the right one? Ever since a certain day of blue skies and summer like this—a long time ago. True enough, he had been able to laugh at himself for it afterwards: the greenest of green students who took it prodigiously seriously when his lady-love was so silly and prudish that she was ashamed to bathe with him. But every time he had chanced to call it to mind—the cliff that rose steeply from the brown waters of the forest lake, the sun-drenched woods and the glistening osier-boughs that waited for his milk-white mistress to emerge from her leafy hiding-place—he had always thought that at that moment the conviction had come to him that their race was descended from an estate called Paradise. But they had had to leave the manor, and he was to learn that it was vain for a boy to attempt to recover the fee-simple.[34]

We have only to think of the fragile tenderness (*ömhet* in Swedish) in the heart of Ingmar Bergman's film *Summer Games* (*Sommarlek*), to see the contemporary extent of the theme of lost paradise, whose reflection reaches us through the fleeting silhouettes in between the trees. The unexplainable and resistant richness of these acts of tenderness between the young student and Maria, as well as the unavoidable threat of death that hovers over them—a stupid accident, everything is gone, and there is no more summer—is a sign which Sigrid Undset herself points out. We are exiles, but traces of the first fire of our loves and friendships constantly come into our minds during those "other days" with their frivolity, that fleetingly cut through the monotony of "days too long."

This is the particular concern in *Gymnadenia*. Within this apparently nearby universe of water, healthy and simple joy, and the lucid knowledge of a world which science has mastered for us, an itinerary is prepared that leads Paul Selmer to where he had neither thought nor wished to go, a place toward which he was being diverted and magnetized by something inside him like the magnetic north of his desire.

From the moment that Lucy and Paul try to live together, something moves them to surpass their too carnal love and to discover a need, a quest and, ultimately, for Paul at least, the faith. This itinerary is an example. Many people today want immediate results. They are immersed in the tangible. They know, as Clamence says in *The Fall*, "what to do in love." They come to say that love is one function among others, just as man is a function in society.

These young men and women, employees of Oslo, live within a universe that is completely closed in upon itself, without any contact with Catholicism (practically non-existent in Norway) or with the Lutheran State Church. They are born into a pagan world. They believe in what they see, and believe only in that. They are sports-minded. In love, they look for a tangible, sensual fullness. They end up by discovering a superior human and religious dimension.

Paul is first haunted by the image of the lost paradise:

> What aggravated his pain and his vague uneasiness was that the image of her young and dazzlingly white form, as she stood before the glistening osier bush with the yellow flowers dotted among the grass at her feet, haunted him day and night. It ought to have belonged to a world in which innocence and beauty were the same, and where he could have dashed forward and thrown his brown, muscular arms about her soft white body, while the sun and the clouds and the lake and the woods were nothing but a garden planted for them.
>
> By the way, he had thought too that the engraving of the fettered Andromeda which hung in his father's drawing-room reminded him of Lucy. So evidently it was tragic images that she recalled—the fettered Andromeda and the wounded Amazon.[35]

This sword in the flesh will not leave him. Long afterward, as a husband and a father, the image of Lucy remains with him:

> Lucy—. It seemed that the more he found out about her, the more there was he did not know. She too was a mysterious thing that he must leave to God. Well, God knows how all this is going to end.[36]

He begins by revolting against this reality, this truth of God:

Why, good heavens, that he had kissed Lucy and told her—as was the truth—that he loved her, that was wrong naturally, but it was only like the little stone that loosens and rolls down, bringing a whole rock-slide with it—till the naked soil is exposed, that one has never seen before. The very foundation of sin: I will be my own master. I will not hear of any indebtedness. After that every man does as he pleases according to the nature he has been given. There are as many as seven deadly sins sitting in a row and waiting for a partner—

He had fallen asleep several times as he knelt there by the sofa, with his arms and face resting on the seat. And he had woke again with the cold and the stiffness of his uncomfortable position, and each time he tried again to pray. But all his praying was only like throwing sand up into the air, it fell back and scattered over himself.

God, Thou hast really been all to me. I have believed Thee to be my saviour and the saviour of the whole world. . . .

And now everything in me is against Thee, because Thou art the truth. And a dream that I myself scarcely believed to be more than a dream, is not true; and what I myself knew to be unreal is not real; and she and I and all men are as Thou hast created us and as sin has marred us; the images we ourselves form of men who do not exist, have no existence.

Thou dost command that we deny ourselves, because we are unreal; and now I would deny Thee because Thou art real, if I could do it.

I will not submit to Thy will, because it is the only one which is a creative will. Is it so hard to have to submit oneself and see that we can only live and act in that which *is*— we cannot create anything which is not?

O God, O God, give me back a little love for Thee, for I cannot bear to believe in Thee, if I do not love Thee—[37]

Soon he will be heard. He will discover that it is in respecting God in the face of each man's freedom, his own freedom, that perhaps the deepest secret of divinity resides. It is to this God who does not defend himself that he ends up by saying "yes." A few days later, while praying in a church, Paul discovers this secret of God:

> God could have forced men to walk in His ways as obediently as the stars. But He enters the world of men, clad in the old habiliments of Adam, and lays aside His omnipotence at the door. The thought took his breath away. It was as though he could see it: the contrast between a universe moving in constant rhythms according to eternal laws and the everlasting lawless tumult of human wills; it was a kind of vision—a glimpse of omnipotence ruling the cosmos and going about begging in the throng of human souls, a beggar who asked to be allowed to give and to deal out some of the mysterious wealth of his own being. As when rays of sunlight suddenly break out from under a thick bank of cloud, lighting up a whole band of glittering points on the surface of inexhaustible mysteries in each shining spot.
>
> There was a darkness in which God had forsaken God. But men He has not forsaken—
>
> Paul lay prostrate before the communion rail. From the realm of unfathomable mysteries and from the real presence a few steps away he felt the will which closed around his will. It swept over him like a flood and he felt himself swallowed up—by that of which fire is a symbol in this world; his soul was blinded by something of which light serves as a token here on earth. It was as though a burning bush drew him into itself, closed around him, consumed him, and yet he continued to exist—then it released him again, then it was no more, but it left behind a paralysing sense of happiness.[38]

This joy is to found beyond what Bergson called pleasure. It is identified with the peace Isaiah speaks of when he says: "Lo, it was in my peace that I knew a most bitter bitterness."

Sigrid Undset's specifically Catholic work includes two high-points: *Kristin Lavransdatter* and *Olav Audunssön* (*The Master of Hestviken*). These novels give us a picture of thirteenth-and fourteenth-century Catholic Norway, and the author wishes to describe the drama of sin and grace. People sin as they breathe in Sigrid Undset's universe: adulteries, murders, brawls, drunkenness, war. We are plunged into a world where sin is taken for granted. People sin by weakness, by being carried off by passion, but also by hatred.[39]

At the end of *Kristin Lavransdatter*, Kristin has lost her husband. Her children are like a swarm of sparrow-hawks, thinking only of leaving home. She asks herself if it was for this that she married her husband, carried, gave birth to and brought up his children. Why did Erlend have to die? Why is she old, with her children thinking only of leaving their home like birds of prey who want to quit the nest as soon as possible?

The plague ravages the whole province of Trondhjem. Kristin, old and abandoned by everyone, participates in the fight against the epidemic. The love she has for her children and for her husband now becomes a universal love, transposing itself into a broader reality. It is directed to all whom she meets; no longer only to those whom she has chosen, but to those who offer themselves to her. She cares for the sick, and no longer has any time to think of herself, to think of her past. She herself becomes infected. Struck down by the sickness that is eventually to take her off, she is brought back to her house. She has the feeling that she lost everything, Erlend, her children, her relatives, but she feels that she is returning to her father's house, the house both of her own father and her Father in heaven.

The young Kristin often rebelled against her parents, for she was stubborn, disobedient, and violent. But she also loved them. Her father knew what his daughter had done: he forgave her without bitterness or resentment. In this existence where people are ill, poor, wicked, good, where children die, are in pain, or laugh, we find an undercurrent of a love which is much more vast and directed toward all men, a brotherly love.

They struggled forward along the sandy track that led across the flat toward the pine wood. The wind swept in freely here, but yet 'twas not as it had been down on the strand, and, as they drew farther and farther way from the roar of the beach, she felt it as a homefaring from the horror of utter darkness. Beside their path the ground showed lighter—'twas a cornfield that there had been none to reap. The scent of it, and the sight of the beaten-down straw, welcomed her home again—and her eyes filled with tears of sisterly pity—out of her own desolate terror and woe she was coming home to fellowship with the living and the dead. . . .

. . . She was borne in someone's arms—'twas Ulf again—but now he seemed to take on for her the semblance of all who had ever borne her up. When she laid her arms about his neck and pressed her cheek against his stubbly throat, 'twas as though she were a child again with her father, but also as though she were clasping a child to her own bosom—And behind his dark head there were red lights, and they seemed like the glow of the fire that nourishes all love.[40]

At the threshold of adolescence, the young Kristin preferred to take the wild road. She had loved Erlend romantically, and advanced the time for their marriage. She had suffered, sinned, wept, lost her children and her husband. She had disobeyed her father, but here she was now, at the end of her life, a little girl again in her father's arms, and at the same time, since there is but one hearth for all loves, she found herself a mother again, hugging a baby in her arms.

Yet, although she rebelled relentlessly against the goad, she also gave in, like the prodigal son who had said he would not go into his father's field but went after all:

The life that ring had wed her to, that she had complained against, had murmured at, had raged at and defied —none the less she had loved it so, both in good days and evil, that not one day had there been when 'twould not have seemed hard to give it back to God, nor one grief that she could have forgone without regret—

. . . It seemed to her to be a mystery that she could not fathom, but which she knew most surely none the less, that

God had held her fast in a covenant made for her without her knowledge by a love poured out upon her richly—and in despite of her self-will, in despite of her heavy, earthbound spirit, somewhat of this love had become *part* of her, had wrought in her like sunlight in the earth, had brought forth increase which not even the hottest flames of fleshly love nor its wildest bursts of wrath could lay waste wholly. A handmaiden of God had she been—a wayward, unruly servant, oftenest an eye-servant in her prayers and faithless in her heart, slothful and neglectful, impatient under correction, but little constant in her deeds—yet had he held her fast in his service, and under the glittering golden ring a mark had been set secretly upon her, showing that she was his handmaid, owned by the Lord and King who was now coming, borne by the priest's anointed hands, to give her freedom and salvation—

. . . Then all things were lost in a dark red mist, and a roar, that first grew fearsomely; but then it died away little by little, and the red mist grew thinner and lighter, and at last 'twas like a fair morning mist ere the sun breaks through, and all sound ceased, and she knew that now she was dying—[41]

The central character of *Olav Audunssön*, Olav, was also carried away by the instinct of wrongdoing. He did not want to confess his sin, and wanted to preserve his respectability. Throughout his whole life he experienced destruction, the destruction of his home and of his life as a man.

Once he asked forgiveness of his sin and received the grace of absolution and did penance, he discovered communion with nature and his fellows again. The drama of sin and death is part of the cosmos.

At the moment of his death, Olav has the feeling that he has never done anything worthwhile. Up to the last minute he remained caught in his sin, in the lie. He tells himself that there is absolutely nothing in his life to reap. In the half-conscious state of his last agony he sees someone. It is his son, Eirik, who had wanted to become a monk but had to give up the idea. He sinned, but he retained a certain candor, a certain transparency, since unlike his father, he never clung to his sins. Olav has the impression that someone is trying to harvest something from his life. Would there really be something there to make up a sheaf of wheat? His son comes to his aid by prayer and by the love that he has for him.

> Olav had lain awake and had heard sentence passed on his own life by the mouth of his son. Meanwhile an image hovered before his vision—it was the frenzy of fever, but not so violent that he did not know it for what it was. He saw a cornfield, overgrown with tares and thistles, willow-herb and brambles—the weeds flaunted their red and yellow flowers in the sun, and the corn was so choked by them that none could tell that the ground had been sown. But out in the field there walked one—sometimes he thought it was his guardian angel, but sometimes it was Eirik—a friend who did not ask whether the dying man had done him wrong, but thought only of gathering up the poor ears of corn that he could save among the thistles. It should not have been so, his life should have been like a cornfield sway-ing clean and bright and ready for the sickle. But one there was who had been able to find a handful of good corn and would lay it in the balance—[42]

Thus St. John Chrysostom could say in a sermon read on Easter Eve in the Orthodox Church: "Now let those who have not fasted also rejoice, for the Lord has risen!"

When salvation has been lived by a soul who takes grace seri-ously, it gradually transfigures the world. A harmony is gradually established between man and other men, between men and the world!

This is quite biblical, since salvation is the reign with Christ under a new heaven and over a new earth. Sigrid Undset describes man's long voyage for us. Beginning with the prison of a materialistic world, through sin and the attachment to sin, but also through the obstinacy of wanting to be saved, her heroes discover a love which surpasses the love of man for a woman in marriage, for it encompasses all whom we meet, all those who are given to us. Finally, this love flows out into a perspective of world transfiguration.

Olav let go his hold of the corner of the men's house. Swaying he walked on without support. A little way up the look-out rock he climbed, but then sank down and lay in a little hollow, where the dry, sun-scorched turf made him a bed.

The immense bright vault above him and the fiord far below and the woods of the shore began to warm as the day breathed forth its colours. Birds were awake in woods and groves. . . . The troops of clouds up in the sky were flushing, and he began to grow impatient of his waiting—

He saw that all about him waited with him. The sea that splashed against the rocks, rowan and birch that had found foothold in the crevices and stood there with leaves still half curled up—now and again they quivered impatiently, but then they grew calm. The stone to which his face was turned waited, gazing at the light from sky and sea.

From the depths of his memory words floated up—the morning song that he had once known. All the trees of the forest shall rejoice before the face of the Lord, for He comes to judge the world with righteousness, the waves shall clap their hands.—He saw that now they were waiting, the trees that grew upon the rocks of his manor, all that sprouted and grew on the land of his fathers, the waves that followed one another into the bay—all were waiting to see judgment passed upon their faithless and unprofitable master. . . .

. . . he must stand forth and could not declare one deed that he had performed from full and unbroken loyalty, nor could he point to one work that he could call well done.— Lord, rebuke me not in thine anger, neither condemn me in thy justice.—

Above him he saw the whole vault of heaven full of white clouds, they stood thick as an immense flock of lambs, but they were folk. They were white and shone with a light which was within them and filled them as sunshine fills the clouds. Slowly gliding they moved high above him, looking down on him—he recognized his mother and certain of the others too, Ingunn was there—

It was the sunrise, he knew that—but it was like a writing. Thus he had stared at the fine pattern of letters on smooth white vellum, until all at once he knew a word—that time when Arnvid tried to teach him to read writing.

Then the very rays from the source of light broke out and poured down over him. For an instant he stared with open eyes straight into the eye of the sun, tried even, wild with love and longing, to gaze yet deeper into God. He sank back in red fire, all about him was a living blaze, and he knew that now the prison tower that he had built around him was burning. But salved by the glance that surrounded him he would walk out unharmed over the glowing embers of his burnt house, into the Vision which is eternal bliss, and the fire that burnt him was not so ardent as his longing—[43]

It has rarely been so well pointed up how all God's works bless him—*Benedicite omnia opera Domini Domino*—how, at the same time, those who were made masters of the earth had abandoned God's cause, fought among themselves, and betrayed God and their fellows. But her work also shows so well how God's love ultimately triumphs, consuming our prison and returning us to communion with him, with our fellows, our brothers, and with the land of men.

God is the "hidden God." He is the "soft breath" before which Elijah veiled his face. He is the burning bush that purifies and consumes but also transforms and conforms us to the image of his Son. He is the one who penetrates the universe with his hidden and powerful presence—"He came to his own home, and his own people received him not"—and who restores it to his light and harmony. God is resurrection.

II. RESURRECTION: CHARLES PÉGUY

With Péguy, salvation integrates all human endeavors that mankind has attempted in the direction of righteousness and love.

Péguy is the poet of Hope:

Dragged along, hanging on the arms of her two big sisters,
who hold her by the hand,
There is little Hope.
She is coming forward.
And in the middle between her two big sisters she looks as if
she is letting herself be dragged along.
Like a child that does not have the strength to walk.
And who is dragged along this road despite herself.
And in reality it is she who makes the others walk.
And who drags them.
For we only work for our children.
And the two grown-ups walk only for their little sister.[44]

This is all very moving, but seems a bit facile. Actually, it is not at all facile, because Péguy wrote these lines in the throes of despair. In a book on Péguy, Henri Guillemin brought to light some very important aspects of Péguy's weakness and despair and of the failure in his personal and literary life.

It was a total failure of his personal career. His home life was a disaster, as we now know. It is one of the reasons why Péguy did not come back to the sacraments, even though he was converted and had rediscovered the Christian faith. His wife had threatened to leave him if he became practising.

Above all, and this is most important, Péguy was obsessed with the ineluctable obsolescence of the ageing individual and of society, *all* society. He realized that the harmonious city, the socialist city, the city whose gates will be closed only when all men have entered, once they have found the justice which was their right, would also grow old and that there was no way to save socialism from that ageing process that leads progressively to death. This reality ruined the myth of progress. Life is not some sort of a stairway which we constantly climb without ever losing our footing, for there is the fact of growing old, the unavoidable descent of ageing mankind, which in the end will die.

He also experienced total failure in his literary career. The periodical *Cahiers de la Quinzaine*, which has now become a collector's item, lost subscribers with each issue. Péguy sold only one copy of *Eve*. His best friends never read it. Romain Rolland put it on his bookshelves and read it only much later. Daniel Halévy, seeing that Jesus not only spoke in the first quatrain but also in the nine-hundredth, declared that he would read it "later."

Yet, Péguy discovered his "catechism." "I took the 'catechism' seriously, and that brought me a long way." He discovered the necessity of saving the temporal, which he loved, and to which he brought his "black Hussars of the Republic" as he told his secularist professors. He took socialism seriously, as well as the Dreyfus affair and social justice. We have merely to leaf through the *Cahiers de la Quinzaine* or the book by Delaporte, which may be the most complete, or André Rousseaux's *Le Prophète Péguy*. Péguy knew that the first charity that one could extend to people was to give them what was their right. But even so, men grow old and die.

He understood the incarnation. In the aging process that leads to death, the only way to prevent the temporal from growing old and to make it return to its origin where it finds the litheness of the birth of dawn ("everything about a beginning is beautiful"), is for God, who is both young and eternal, to enter into the temporal. Youth is God's own eternity, despite the fact that in the classics youth is bound up with the theme of transitoriness. The wisdom of the nations has said it. And Ronsard said: "Cueillez dès aujourd'hui les roses de la vie, cueillez dès aujourd'hui, n'attendez à demain. (Pluck today the roses of life, pluck them today, wait not till the morrow.)"

Péguy's character Eve has an acute awareness of this waning, this drying up, this progressive ageing process. She is the symbol of the Woman, the Wife, the Mother, the woman who has cared for so many dead sons of man, the woman who has closed the eyes of so many dead men, the woman who attempts to arrange things and put them in order. "Woman, I tell you, you would tidy up God himself," as Péguy says. Eve is constantly mindful of the plenitude from which she comes, of that first garden in which Adam's youth (and the youth of mankind, had Adam accepted God) would have been constantly refreshed and renewed, would have been constantly the cycle of the seasons, as described by Péguy at the beginning of his poem. Jesus is speaking:

O mother buried outside the primeval garden,
Afterwards you never knew that climate of grace
And the round basin and the spring and the lofty terrace

And that first sun shining in the first morn. . . .

You never knew the passionate corn of wheat
In movement at the onslaught of the unending plains.
And the wheat upon its pedestal and the blessings of the
    harvest.
And the stock-taking of the respectable sheaves. . . .

A creation in birth and without memory
Turning and twisting to the curves of the same orb.
And the beech-nut and the acorn and the quince and the
    rowan
More succulent to the taste than the plum and the pear.

God himself bending over everlasting love
Again saw it flower in poor hamlets.
A Father, he thought of a maternal love
Doubly shared between fine twins.

And creation was like a tower
That rose above a vast palace.
And time and space assured contact
And the days of happiness were like one day.[45]

God, who is both young and eternal, is in a state of eternal
renewal. In the heart of the poem, in stanzas added later, Péguy
spoke about this renewal of God. The triune God is a life in an
incessant renewal. It constantly returns to its own heights. This
two- and threefold interchange in God causes God's being constantly to grow, return to its source, and spring back into the
eternity of the very youth of God, while man's being unceasingly decreases.

> You know that God alone gives of Himself,
> And that man's being unceasingly decreases.
>
> And that God's being unceasingly ascends
> To its life-level upon the same height,
> And of itself produces its own double
> And its eternal force and its exactness.

And that God's being unceasingly grows again
To its life-level upon the same height,
And of itself produces its own tripling
And its eternal life and its blessedness.

And that God's being unceasingly turns about
Its eternal source and its plenitude,
And of itself produces its own growth
And its eternal force and its gentleness.

And that God's being unceasingly goes back
To its eternal source and its deep night,
And of itself produces its own growth
and its eternal force and its gentleness.

And that God's being unceasingly goes back
To its eternal source and its deep night,
And of itself produces its own growth
And man's salvation and the world's strength.[46]

Eve remembers this all. She incessantly wants to put things in order. This is the story of our civilizations, the heritage from Israel and the Roman world. Eve knows that she will never *really* be able to put things back in order, to make man's being ascend again to its source, because his being is constantly fading. This is the meaning of the sequence on the resurrection of the dead: "when the resurrected will go out through the towns—still agape," everything will be overturned and topsy-turvy.

When all that is heard is the muffled crackle
Of a world falling to pieces,
When the globe is like a pile of shacks
Full of disuse and lewdness;

When the vast house of the living and the dead
Can show nothing but its decrepitude,
When the ancient debate of the weak and the strong
Can show nothing but its exactitude;

When man will go off into the solemn night,
Still quite giddy at having gone back,

Still quite bewildered at being so poor and naked
Still quite bundled up in his carnal wrap;

When they have passed before the blacksmith
And the forge and the anvil and the secular arm,
When they collide at the corner of a fruit-wall
Still quite sleepy and ill recognizing

Those paths that brought about their naive coarseness,
And when they tremble in this last decease,
Can you bring a lamp to light their steps,
In this uncertainty and in this weakness,

And when they pass beneath the old postern,
Will you have found for these urchins of the streets,
And for these veterans and these young recruits,
Some old lantern to light their steps;

Will you have found in your diminished strength
The little needed to lead this troop
And to lead this funeral and to lead this group
In the joining up of vanished roads?[47]

In the incarnation, God "both young and eternal" becomes "internal" in the sphere of time. He enters into the temporal, inserts himself within it in such a close, placentary, and medullary way that the temporal becomes "temporally eternal." This is a paradox. The temporal apparently fades, apparently grows old, apparently disappears, but it unceasingly renews itself at the source by the presence of God in the incarnation of his son Jesus Christ.

Therefore, the temporal is capable of arresting its decline. It can resuscitate. This is why Péguy writes at the end of the second part of *Eve* "For the supernatural is itself carnal." This is more than merely a fine thought, it is a theological truth.

For[48] the supernatural is itself carnal
And the tree of grace has deep roots
And plunges down into the soil and searches deep
And the tree of the race is itself eternal

And eternity itself is in the temporal
And the tree of grace has deep roots
And plunges down into the soil and touches deep
And time itself is an intemporal time.[49]

"And time itself is a time intemporal": how better to say that time, apparently set in its law of waning and ageing, renews itself at its source incessantly in Christ, ascends to its fulness, to its break of dawn that is temporal and eternal?

And the tree of grace and the tree of nature
Have bound their two trunks with such solemn knots,
They so mingled their fraternal destinies
That they are the same essence and the same height.

And it is the same blood coursing through two veins,
And it is the same sap and the same vessels,
And it is the same honor accruing in two efforts
And it is the same lot sealed with the same seals.

It is the same destiny that runs in two fortunes.
And it is the same death that dies in both deaths.
And it is the same fright that runs through both anxieties.
And the same calm in the bosom of these two ports.

And one will not perish without the other dying.
And one will not survive without the other living.
And one will not remain without the other staying.
And the other will not pass over the supreme bank

Without the other making a like journey.
And one will not leave in its last full dress
Without the other also getting under way
And also embarking on an ultimate voyage.[50]

This incarnation is not only that of Jesus in Palestine. It is continued by the sacraments. This is precisely what Péguy shows in *The Mystery of the Charity of Joan of Arc*, when Joan exclaims: "Oh, my God, how lucky they were who saw Jesus in Palestine!" ... "Everything comes, Lord, but your kingdom! ... Send us a saint, a saint who succeeds!"

Succeed. . . . That means to give bread to those who have
none, to see to it that the poor, to whom she gave her daily
bread but who will be hungry again tomorrow, will have bread
tomorrow. This bottomless abyss of human need is above all this
ageing process from which no one can save anyone except God.
Then Madame Gervaise answers Joan:

> He is here
> He is here as on the first day. . . .
> He is here among us all the days of his eternity. . . .
> A parish shone with an everlasting brightness, but all the
> parishes shine eternally, for in all the parishes there is the
> body of Jesus Christ.
> The same sacrifice crucifies the same body, the same sacri-
> fice causes the same blood to flow.
> Jews . . . Israel . . . but you too, Christians, you do not
> realize your greatness; your present greatness; which is the
> same greatness.
> Your everlasting greatness.[51]

Péguy uses this theme again in *Eve* when he shows us that
Christ's blood, which is the blood of God temporally present
in the world and in our history, is the blood of Calvary and the
blood of the altar. Through the sacraments it is the young and
eternal God who is present in the temporal and raises it.

God is internal by being in the very marrow of the temporal.
Péguy rediscovered the presence of this young and eternal God
in the temporal through the sacraments, and especially the
Eucharist. He rediscovered an absolutely elementary doctrine.
This presence of God in the temporal consecrates the temporal
and does not cause it to evaporate. It saves it by returning its
whole structure to it.

In *Le Mystère des Saints Innocents*, Péguy was obsessed by
childhood, by those who have not had time to become wrinkled
and lose their never to be retrieved spontaneity. At the end of
Eve, he abandons this still rather romantic theme of youth which
has but one "tense." He surpasses it. He shows the two parallel
deaths of Saint Joan of Arc, who died at nineteen, and Saint
Genevieve, who died at 96 (he calls her "young and guileless
dean,") and points out that youth and old age have equal value

in God, for they are taken up into something much more profound, which is the youth of God.

The whole of life is thereby preserved. The last verses of *Eve*
are the most beautiful Péguy has ever written. He shows us God,
the same God we saw at the beginning, "young and eternal,"
inclining toward his creation, toward human existence. A series
of verses begins with the words: "God does not know. . . ." He
does not know which he should love more, an existence cut off
in its youth or an existence harvested in August. In a beautiful
life, there are only beautiful days. God looks at its whole extent
and looks for a long time to see which is the most beautiful of
all these loves.

> And since we do not know when a year is good
> What we love best, whether it is the hard summer,
> Or the melancholy and yellowing autumn,
> And since we do not know when the lot is cast . . .
>
> And since we do not know when a year is beautiful
> What we love best, whether it is the sudden showers
> Or whether it is the return of the black swallow
> Or whether it is the network of unrolled troubles,
>
> .   .   .   .
>
> So God does not know among so many fine days
> What he loves best, whether it is the fresh spring,
> Or the severity of stauncher loves,
> Or the declivity of times more oblique.
>
> .   .   .   .
>
> So God does not know among so many fine days
> What he loves best, whether it is young childhood
> Or whether it is work and games and dancing
> Or the fidelity of earthly loves.
>
> .   .   .   .
>
> In a beautiful life there are only fine days.
> In a beautiful life the weather is always fine.

God unrolls it completely and looks long
For what love is dearest among all these loves.[52]

This brings us to an essential doctrine: salvation is the resurrected Christ. We receive him in the Eucharist, which is the risen Christ in his humanity. This humanity of the risen Christ in us is the leaven of our body's resurrection, of that of our whole being, and it will permit us to enter into the Kingdom of God where we shall reign with Christ.

Péguy finally discovered that this insertion, this incarnation is painful. It is bound up with death. In the excised verses of *Eve* (which are still to be found in the Pléiade edition) Péguy speaks of Christ's side pierced with a lance. This piercing of Christ's heart is at the origin of the birth of the Church, a traditional symbol which Péguy rediscovered almost miraculously.

The lance pierced Christ's heart and opened it so that a new Eve, the Church, might come forth. Onto this image of the soldier piercing Christ's heart he superimposes the figure of the glass of a great rotunda, cracked in one place by a pebble. The crack spreads out in a circumscribed circle. Upon this he superimposes still a third: the Roman roads, those roads of civilization created by the Romans which were a preparation for the coming of Christ. Christ inherited them, since the missionaries went along them bringing the message of the resurrection. The two figures of the lance that pierced the heart of Christ and the pebble that cracked the immense rotunda mean that the lance also pierced the heart of Rome. The Church, which is Christ present among us according to the Spirit in the sacrament of the Eucharist, is a Church in pain. The Rome he gives us is not the baroque Rome with its temporal triumph, but a wounded, suffering Rome. What goes out from Rome into the body of Christ is the humanity of a "young and eternal" God, of a God who died for us.

The soldier's lance piercing Jesus' side is compared to the throwing (in French: *lancer*) of a rock at the glass of an immense rotunda, causing cracks to run round through it. Thus, from this pierced heart will grow the network of arteries and roads through which the redemptive blood will come to save, renew, and raise the world. The insertion of the temporal into the eternal, in the heart of Jesus, comes about through pain and death.

Those roads that went off and turned the world
By their splintering into a starred mirror,
Those roads that carried a vagabond soul
To the ends of an exiled land.

As if the world had been cracked by a rock,
Its star spreading out from Rome,
Like the crystal of an immense rotunda
Starred from the blow of one man.

. . . .

As if the world had been struck by a lance
Just as the side of Christ was stricken,
The cracks became a deep star
With rays of an inscribed and circumscribed circle.

And as if the Roman spear and language
Had come down again in the very heart of Rome
Just as human terror and distress
Came down again into the very heart of man.[53]

III. UNITY

1. PAUL CLAUDEL AND THE TREE OF THE CROSS

The unity theme is at the center of Claudel's work. Saving the
world means bringing into it justice and love. To save men is to
fasten their common bonds of knowledge and birth, which root
and solder them into a vast functioning people. To save men is
to refasten the marriage bond between them and the universe
entrusted to them by God. Claudel's heroes, Tête d'Or, Pierre
de Craon, Rodrigo, Colomb, are "musterers" of the earth. Man
is in the image of God, which means that he must dominate
over the earth and make it a human world, while at the same
time his humanity becomes earthly, cosmic, participating in
the great movements of the planetary tide. In our time of an
expanding universe, and a quest for unity, it is good to present
salvation as a harmony between peoples and the "immense

octave of creation." This is the direction announced by the
Word of God in the Bible.

We first find Claudel's hero in the character Cébès. Obsessed
with death, obsolescence, and vagrancy, we find him here at the
threshold of Claudel's greatest and richest drama:

I stand here,

Untaught, irresolute,

A man new-born confronting things unknown.

I turn my face towards the Future and the lowering arch of
the sky. My soul is full of weariness!

I know nothing. There is nothing I can do. What shall I say?
What shall I do?

How shall I use these hands that hang at my sides, these feet

That bear me about as in a dream?

Speech is but a noise and books are only paper.

There is no one here but myself. And all that is about me,

The foggy air, the rich fields,

The trees, the low-lying clouds

Seem to speak to me, soundlessly, to ask inarticulate
questions.

The ploughman

Turns homeward with his plough. I hear its slow creaking.

It is the time when women bring water from the wells.

It is night.—What am I?

What am I doing? For what do I wait?

And I answer, "I do not know!"

And in my heart there is a wild desire

To weep or to cry aloud

Or to laugh or leap in the air and wave my arms!

"Who am I?"

There are still some patches of snow. I hold in my hand a
sprig of pussy-willow.

For March is like a woman blowing a fire of green wood.

—That the Summer

And the dreadful day under the glare of the sun may be forgotten,

O Nature,
Here I offer myself to you!
I know so little!
Look at me! There is something that I need.
But what it is I do not know and I could cry forever
Loud and low like a child that one hears in the distance, like
    children left alone beside the glowing embers!
O lowering sky! Trees, earth, darkness, night of rain!
Look upon me! Grant my prayer![54]

This incomparable beginning expresses the anguish of a person
who wants to be everything, and does not even know whether
he exists, while the March cold covers the rich, overladen, and
damp ground with bird-lime and haze. During these years,
Claudel had seen his grandfather die of cancer. Death obsessed
him as he describes in *Tête d'Or*. Simon Agnel, who has met
Cébès, comes back in the second act, victorious like the rising
sun. But he is unable to restore life to the dying Cébès:

For I am like a man buried alive, and I am confined as in an
    oven!
Give me light! Give me light! Give me light! Give me light!
    For I would see!
Give me air, for I stifle!
Give me to drink, for I do not want the water that they bring
    me.
But you, give me water to drink, that I may die in peace, for
    I am consumed with thirst!
O brother! I have put my trust in you! Will you not help
    me? I beg you, soldier, head of gold, O my bright-haired
    brother![55]

Tête d'Or cannot save his friend from death. It is possibly the
obsession with this basic failure that gives a nobility worthy of
Aeschylus to the cosmic adventure that will lead him up to
the height of the Caucasus. Tête d'Or cannot save himself alone.
He needs the whole earth, like a tree which needs the earth for
its roots and the vault of heaven for its branches. This tree
image, I think, is primary in Claudel's universe. It serves as a

title for the collection of his first four plays (*L'Arbre*), and is expressed very clearly in the first act of *Tête d'Or:*

> O tree, receive me again! Alone I left the protection of your branches. And now it is alone that I return, O immovable father!
>
> Take me once more beneath your shadow, O son of the Earth! O wood, in this hour of sorrow! O murmuring branches, impart to me
>
> That message which I am and of which I feel within me the terrible striving.
>
> For you yourself are only a ceaseless striving, the unwearied drawing of your body out of inanimate matter.
>
> How you suck the earth, old tree,
>
> Thrusting down, stretching out in every direction your strong and subtile roots! And the sky, how you cling to it! How your whole being breathes it in through one great leaf, Form of Flame!
>
> The inexhaustible earth in the grasp of all the roots of your being
>
> And the infinite sky, with the sun, with the stars in their constellations,
>
> Of which you lay hold with that mouth made of all your arms, with the cluster of your branches, with the clutch of all there is in you that breathes.
>
> All the earth and all the sky, these are what you require that you may hold yourself erect!
>
> Let me also hold myself erect! Let me not lose my soul! That essential sap, that innermost secretion of my ego, that effervescence
>
> Which constitutes my true self, oh let me not squander that to make a useless tuft of leaves and flowers! Let me grow in my unity! Let me remain unique and erect!
>
> But it was not to hear your murmuring that I came,
>
> O branches that now are bare mid the air opaque and nebulous!

> But it is you that I would question, deep-reaching roots and
> that primal depth of the earth where you are nourished.[56]

The soul he wants to save is not the small, volatile, and dis-
incarnate substance that a pseudo-Christianity (what Nietzsche
calls "Platonism for the people") could pass off as the work of
the Creator of the "first man" who was made a "living soul."
This soul is concrete, bound up with the substance of the sap,
the liquor which is so much part of the tree that feeds and the
branches that rustle. We see a new subtle correlation between
the texts of St.-John Perse and the early Claudel. The "horse's
soul" of the Prince in *Anabasis* is not far from this "soul, this
essential sap" of *Tête d'Or*.

Claudel will discover that the only tree that can assure possession of the world, this plucking of the "perfect apple," earth,
is the tree of the cross. Having arrived at the heights of the
Caucasus, Tête d'Or is already mortally wounded in the thigh,
and he will die in the great blaze of the sun. Like a new
Prometheus, he dies in a kind of Dionysiac ecstasy:

> O Father,
> Come! O Smile, recline upon me.
> As the folk of the vintage before the vats
> Go out from the house of the wine-press by all the doors like
>   a torrent,
> My blood by all these wounds goes out to meet you in
>   triumph.
> I die. Who shall relate
> That dying, arms outstretched, I held the sun on my breast
> like a wheel?[57]

But there is another wound that tears at him. It was given
him by a woman, the mysterious princess whom Tête d'Or
loves. He does not yet know what this love means, since it is so
different from the appetite for possessing the perfect apple, and
yet it is so mysteriously joined with it. At the moment of death,
he sees her nearby:

> No, woman! You cannot
> Take this life in your hair.

Live! Be queen! All that I have I leave to you.

Mortal man,

As a traveller benighted in bitter cold takes refuge in the
    entrails of his horse,

Comforts himself with his woman, seizing her by the breast.

But as for me, I do not desire you.

Let me die alone!

Once more

Like a flame there rolls

In my breast the great desire.

Ah!

The child of my mother

Has been enmeshed in a whirling fury, as his face is enmeshed
    by the soft and terrestrial flame of his hair;

But now I, a better mother, I myself like a rigid son, shall
    give birth to a hairy soul!

I hope! I hope! I aspire.

You cannot undo this tough soul with your woman's nails.

Again it fills its iron harness.[58]

"I hope, I aspire":[59] in French, there is a play on words here
pointing up the incarnational character that salvation has for
Claudel. To hope is to aspire with one's whole self to the possession of the world that God willed for man by creating him
in his image. To hope does not mean a kind of retirement within one's own lukewarm wishes, and a turning of one's back on
the cold and bloody fact of reality. It is to share totally in this
great aspiration, this nursing function of which the tree is the
symbol.

In this first work of his, mingled with mankind's aspiration
to possess the world, we also see the failure of this possession,
and the mysterious presence of the mystery woman, the promise
that "cannot be kept." Death is total. Love is a kind of hook
that tears us from ourselves, opens us up and wounds us fatally.
These are the two ways of access that will lead Claudel's characters to rediscover the one tree that can deliver captive souls
and launch them on the great adventure of the ingathering of
the universe, of the great ordering of all things mute and
speaking.

*   *   *

We know that Claudel, like St. Paul on the road to Damascus, was stricken by God's grace. We should like to give a short account of this conversion, since in it we can see the action of grace which in this instance seems almost to rise out of its anonymity.

This was the unhappy child who on December 25, 1886, made his way to Notre-Dame de Paris for the Christmas services. I had begun at that time to write and it had seemed to me that in the Catholic ceremonies (which I looked down upon from the point of view of a superior dilettantism) I would find something to excite me and the material for a few symbolist compositions. It is with these dispositions, elbowed and pushed about by the crowd, that I assisted with a modicum of pleasure at the Solemn Mass. Later, having nothing better to do, I came back for Vespers. The choir boys in white robes and the pupils from the minor seminary of Saint-Nicolas-du-Chardonnet who augmented them were in the process of singing what I later found out was the *Magnificat.* I was standing in the crowd near the second pillar at the entrance to the choir on the right of the sacristy side. And it was at that moment that I experienced an event that has dominated my whole life. In a twinkling of an eye my heart was touched and *I believed.* I believed with such an adhering force, such an exaltation of my whole being, such a powerful conviction, and such certainty that left no place for doubt, that afterwards all the books, all the reasoning, all the hazards of a tumultuous life were unable to shake my faith, nor truthfully speaking even to touch it. All at once I had the excruciating feeling of innocence, the eternal infancy of God, an unspeakable revelation. In trying, as I have often done, to reconstruct the minutes that followed this extraordinary moment, I find the following elements that are, however, but one lightning-bolt, one weapon used by Providence to reach and open the heart of a poor despairing child: "How happy are people who believe! And if it really were true? It is true! God exists. He is there. He is someone, a being as personal as I! He loves me, and is calling me."[60]

I am not going to give any detailed comment on this text since each word seems to hold up by itself like a building constructed with blocks but without cement. Father Blanchet has done so, however, in a masterly way.[61] I should merely like to emphasize the overwhelming nature of what happened but especially the very close connection that is shown between the revelation of a truth and a personal call. In the same shower of fire Claudel discovered the truth of God, "God's eternal childhood," and felt in the depth of his heart an irresistible call. In conversion, light is always bound up with the heat of the fire that dissolves and recomposes.

In the commentaries on this great text it seems to me that there has not been enough emphasis on the initial content of the revelation of God as a personal reality. Claudel had this excruciating feeling of innocence, the eternal infancy of God. Here conjoined we find both the Old Testament theme of God renewing our youth and an almost mystical intuition of God's innocence, his non-defense, similar to that of a child who without any visible weapons offers himself to our love and also to our hatred or our disdain. It seems remarkable to me that this savage and hungry being that the young Claudel was (people called him a hot-headed young bull) could have had a revelation of God as eternal childhood. This soft and secret pulp was to remain in all of his work. It came gradually to infiltrate the iron muscles of Claudel's heroes. This is what saves his work from becoming baroque in the style of Santa Maria della Vittoria. We need only to think of the intolerable scene in *The Satin Slipper* where Doña Musica prays in a Prague church after the slaughter of the Battle of the White Mountain.

Claudel fought four years against the compelling experience he had that Christmas in 1886:

The edifice of my opinions and my attainments remained standing and I saw nothing defective in it. It had only happened that I had come out of it. A new and formidable being revealed itself, with dreadful exigencies for the young man and artist that I was, and I did not know how to reconcile it with anything of my surroundings. The state of a man torn from his skin and planted in an alien body in the midst of an unknown world is the only comparison I can find to express this complete distress.[62]

The young poet defended himself at every step, as did all his heroes.

*   *   *

Yet a crack had been made, tender and hidden. It was God's apparent weakness, which is true power. It was to lead his heroes, and undoubtedly also to some extent the poet himself, to the possession of the world, in a state of total abjection.

The most beautiful play of Claudel after *Tête d'Or* (its first version and not the glossed up version prepared for the stage), is *Break of Noon*. The hero (and we know that Claudel put much in it from his own personal drama) is taken with a woman who is forbidden to him, since she is the wife of a friend. The final scene of the third act, as we wait for the explosion that is to blow up the hut in which Mésa had taken refuge, symbolizes the force of the disintegration of the whole of society and world order which is hidden beneath adulterous love. Yet how heart-rending for a proud heart must have been the snatching away of the woman after he had been joined with her in the burning ardor of noon. *Break of Noon*: in the midst of life's road, sacrifices weigh heavier, for we know better that life is short and God is silent—a silence that is the complement of his Word. How many deserts there are to cross in order to perceive this soft breeze which harbors the whole power of God in its presence! It is this "unkept promise" that teaches Mésa that he is excluded from the universe. The expected final explosion symbolizes the splintering off of a portion of ground that no longer wants anything to do with one who has cut himself off from his roots by following his personal law. But this explosion is also the breaking down within him of those walls that stood in the way of salvation. As Paul-André Lesort says so well: "It is not on the side roads but on the direct route that Mésa is stricken. It is the possibility of being self-sufficient that is destroyed in him in a flash. It is man's own will that is reached by the fire, because man is finally broken, severed in the middle, like a broken eggshell. The Mésa who believes that he knows how to give of himself, a big pebble that has only to change scenery, is the one struck by lightning. Uncreated love reaches him in the flash of created love. If God were not love, love would then be more than God."[63]

In the middle of *The Satin Slipper*, in this same dazzlement of created love (Rodrigo's love for Prouheze), the lightning of un-created love reaches the Conquistador who wants to unite the New World and join it to the Old. As the guardian angel says to Prouheze, in the breaking off of this love demanded of her, Rodrigo will rejoin the universe, come to the cosmic tree, and this time in a state of total abjection:

> He joins up with the other world as before, having taken it in rear.
>
> Here they suffer and wait. And behind that partition, as high as the sky, above, below, begins the other slope, the world from which he comes, the Church Militant.
>
> He is going to survey those kneeling populations, those enclosed and dense-packed regions which are looking not for a way out, but for their center.
>
> One in the shape of a triangle and the other of a circle.
>
> And the other is those torn islands endlessly tormented with storm and fire.
>
> India hangs done to a turn in scorching vapour, China for ever in that inmost laboratory where water turns to mud, tramples down that slime mingled with her own scourings.
>
> And the third is tearing herself with rage.
>
> Such are those peoples groaning and awaiting, facing towards the rising sun.
>
> 'Tis to them he is sent as ambassador.
>
> He bears with him enough sin to understand their darkness.
>
> God has shown him joy enough for him to understand their despair.
>
> That nothingness on whose brink they have sat so long, that Void made by the absence of Being, played upon by the reflex of heaven, he had to bring them God to make them understand it quite.

It is not Rodrigo that is bringing God, but he must come so that the lack of God in which those multitudes are lying may be looked into.[64]

Rodrigo has lost a leg in his battles for the King of Spain; he is in disgrace at court, abandoned by everyone. At the end of the fourth day he is accepted, by the almswoman of "Mother Teresa," as the porter of a Carmelite convent, and the cry that closes the drama rings out: "Deliverance for the captive souls!" This is the moment of Rodrigo's marriage with the stars, with the ocean, with those far countries that await the mark of man and God. . . . This is the moment, in the silent rocking of the boat where the helpless old man is taken on as an extra hand, when we perceive the lurching of the whole of creation, restored to God in grace by the hands of man.

I know of no more beautiful image than that of the daughter of Doña Prouheze swimming to meet John of Austria, with the ironic counterpoint of the butcher's daughter drowning. At times *The Satin Slipper* becomes very heavy, but the flow of these verses restores the fragile but inexorable and powerful throb of grace that reconciles in unity. Sevenswords is speaking to the unfortunate butcher's daughter, who soon will no longer hear her:

Let us go now quietly at our ease. It is delightful to soak in this kind of liquid light that makes us into hovering godlike beings, (*in thought*) glorified bodies.

No more need of hands to grasp with or feet to carry you.

You go on, like the sea-anemone's breathing, by the mere expansion of the body and the kick of the will.

The whole body is one sense, a planet watching the other planets in the air.

(*Aloud*)

I feel immediately with my heart every beat of thy heart.

(*Here, the* BUTCHER'S DAUGHTER *drowns.*)

The water bears up everything. It's delightful, your ear on a level with the water, to notice all those melting musics (*in thought*)—the dancers around the guitar.

Life, songs, words of love, the incalculable crackle of all those whispered words!

And all that is no longer outside one, you are inside; there is something that unites you blissfully with everything, a drop of water mingling with the sea! The Communion of Saints![65]

This incantation makes a transfigured world almost tangible. It has lost its heaviness and its opaqueness but not its reality. Here we find again the lyricism of *L'Esprit et l'Eau*, but with a tonality that is nocturnal and appeased, where the water becomes a song and the bodies luminous and musical crystals. It is very remarkable to see how starting with the figure of the cosmic tree we end up with the water image, that primordial symbol in which Claudel saw the "playful element" that reconciles, brings together and vivifies. The hidden pulp of eternal childhood appears here in the ecstatic and naive chatter of Doña Sevenswords. Yet the heaviness of the earth is not overlooked with the drowned butcher's daughter! To the strongly masculine element that was dominant in his first works we see joined the fluid and musical harmony that is ever present: the tree, an assertive force, a verticality that wants to penetrate and ascend, to clutch the sky and the earth in a muscular thrust; and the water, which flows, glides, seeps in, washes, and ultimately fecundates and reconciles.

Actually, it is "our sister death," and also love, the awesome love of a man for a woman, this mysterious call of a woman to a man, which lead Claudel's heroes to find salvation, the unity of the possession of the world in their self-effacement. Claudel's Christopher Columbus, broken and deprived of everything, must still give away the only thing remaining of his glory, the old run-down horse that even a Don Quixote would no longer want. It is at this point that he becomes aware of the soaring hope of the ingathering of the universe.

2. GERTRUD VON LE FORT AND THE TORMENT OF UNITY

Claudel's work runs the risk of making us "set out for glory." His baroque style, which is what is most original in his work (much more than the superimposed medievalism of *The Tidings Brought to Mary*), is in constant danger of toppling over, in a more wordy than availing anticipation of the real unity of the world.

On the other hand, Gertrud von Le Fort has a sense of unity that is at once deeper and more concrete than Claudel's. For our purposes she provides us with an indispensable complement. If Claudel's lush lyricism makes us forget at times that "God's ways are not pathways," Gertrud von Le Fort prevents us from forgetting it. In reading her, one particular idea stands out: no one knows when the Kingdom of God will come about in its fullness. The dimension of the expectation of salvation is penetrated with hope and eschatological patience in this excellent body of work, which is too little known.

There is "breathing" in every line of Gertrud von Le Fort's writing, as well as the unshakable expectation of unity and the crucifying experience that no human force can fill up the abyss separating men. This is why we have chosen to conclude our book with her work. It is balanced between a hope that asserts that there will be unity and the tragedy of our political, religious, and Christian differences, and therefore it corresponds somewhat to the work of Kafka, our witness to the "promised land." It undoubtedly surpasses Péguy's, since its notion of salvation is more vast.

Gertrud von Le Fort's family was Protestant and came from Savoy, which they were obliged to leave after the revocation of the Edict of Nantes in 1685. They emigrated to Russia (where a part of the family still lives) and to Poland, and from there they returned through Mecklenburg to northern Germany. Because of her family history, Gertrud von Le Fort was obsessed by the theme of unity. Her father was a Kantian type of Protestant, her mother a pietistic Lutheran. She herself joined the Roman Catholic Church in 1926.

a) *Political Unity*

Gertrud von Le Fort was deeply imbued with the idea of an empire, a *Reich*, a collective unity that ought to encompass all men under one government of peace, righteousness, and justice. Through her studies at Heidelberg and the story of her family, she knew that this political unity is the most necessary and at the same time the most inaccessible thing for the world today. She remained deeply convinced that it was impossible to bring about such an earthly empire. To try to do so produces cataclysms like the last two world wars.

In her novel *The Veil of Veronica* (which includes two parts:

The Roman Fountain and *The Wreath of Angels*), Enzio, a German and a militant atheist, wants to create a new *Reich* in which there will be no defeats, only crowns of victory. Enzio wants to reject the crown of thorns of which his convert fiancée, Veronica, constantly reminds him. He tells her that in his kingdom there will be only crowns of victory. There will be no conquered people, only the victorious.

In this imperial ideology we must go toward a political unity of justice and charity which will eliminate conflicts and wars in the entire world. All approximations of this unity are valid. Yet, the error begins from the moment that we wish to "fasten the buckle," which necessarily implies that violent means, war and tyranny, will be utilized. Once again, injustice will prevail.

On earth, there is no question of ever making a perfect political unity a reality. All that we can do is to produce approximations and symbols of unity. We cannot speed up the time of history, which is also God's time.

b) *Religious Unity*

Religious unity is the second aspect of salvation. Gertrud von Le Fort is conscious of the presence in the world today of both atheists and believers. It seems impossible to build a bridge between them, to hope, humanly speaking of course, that unbelievers will come to believe. This does not mean that we should not preach the Gospel to them, that we must not be missionaries. It is only that Gertrud von Le Fort has understood that there are people who are born outside of Christianity, outside of religious faith. They are in good faith in their atheism. There is a mystery in atheism and unbelief. The Christian must become aware of the fact that he is living in a pluralistic world where there are atheists.

The generation of students described by the author no longer believes in metaphysics. Paul Valéry's intellectual Hamlet becomes a skeptical and violent group of students. Enzio says sarcastically to Veronica that there is no longer any need for metaphysics, no matter what its species, and he makes his own this ironic thought:

> There is metaphysics when you have a man born blind, in a perfectly dark room, looking for a completely black cat, which, furthermore, is absolutely just not there.[66]

Veronica had known her fiancé in Rome. He was a young poet, despondent, but not yet the hate-filled atheist that she was to discover at Heidelberg after the First World War. The evening of the same day, Enzio and Veronica are together:

Then he became indignant. Why was I constantly speaking to him about someone who represented my father? The younger generation had no need of such a substitute. They no longer *have* any father. They've renounced him [*ihre Väter hätten versagt*]. And yet I belong to his generation. He won't take any order from the professor, especially in regard to his future life. This is the most important thing that concerns him. He [Veronica's tutor] has got it into his head once and for all that he [Enzio] and especially he, ought to be his scientific heir. His mind has become so deeply involved in its own direction that he hasn't the slightest hint about what is going on today.[67]

Once again, from one author to another, themes overlap and reoccur. Sartre's characters also rejected paternal values. Here we hear of a "fatherless generation." With the awful disillusionment of youth faced with their fathers' "failure," we have the intermingling of resentment and rejection.

Veronica is both deeply Christian and deeply in love with Enzio. As her friend Jeanette tells her, she is not one of those who pass hurriedly along the sidelines of the world.

"As with everything coming from God you wanted to embrace this event with enthusiasm! In other words, you did not want to hurry through this world with your face turned away but to remain in it, share its joys and its sufferings, truly live with it, win its confidence—and all full of joy according to the word: 'Royal messenger, do your service with gladness'; for, as you wrote me, after all you are sent to the world as a royal messenger."[68]

Veronica's tutor represents the great current of German liberalism which loves Christian civilization but without having the faith. This person, in whom the author has put some characteristics of her former Heidelberg professor, Tröltsch, perceives acutely the gravity of the crisis: this young generation of intellectuals will destroy everything. He says as much to Veronica:

> This boy will destroy our whole culture. And he will destroy you too. Let him go, as quickly as possible. It's the only advice I can give you.[69]

He knows quite well that to save this Christian civilization, more than erudition and concern are necessary. People need faith. For erudition and an attachment to "Christian Europe" are merely like the light of dusk. They do not warm, nor can they ripen new fruit. He answers Veronica simply:

> No, this power I don't have. Dusk may transfigure but it no longer ripens any fruit. Respect for the Christian faith and knowledge in depth about it can never replace total faith. I shall not be capable of saving the culture. I shall merely go down with it, flag unfurled, but at least without any cowardly compromise.[70]

But he sees in Veronica one who will be able to save what is essential in the patrimony, for she has faith. And at the same time she "loves" this modern world which is no longer Christian:

> You have shown me how a genuine and alive Christian bond with God is connected also with what we call the world. I mean with the values of the past. You accept these values with indescribable enthusiasm, yet you are ready to give up everything as a sacrifice for your bond with God, even your happiness, while everywhere else the contrary is happening. Everyone is having little trouble sacrificing religious values for trifles. They're not even aware of what they're doing, so little do these values even exist for them.[71]

Veronica's love for Enzio is of this kind. She has loved him since those moments lived together in Rome: in the Forum, when she had had the intuition of a world that was going to collapse and crumble in chaos; at the Colosseum, when by moonlight she suddenly saw the profile of a sterile, dead, and accursed world; and again in the Roman countryside, when she listened to Enzio's despairing and lush poetry; and finally, during the hours at Heidelberg, on the slopes near the castle hidden in the forest. What she loves in him is the sad young poet, the strong and dark prince who is going to found an empire without defeats and without crowns of thorns. She also loves in him the mystery of despair, of the resentment that feeds his incredulousness. But she loves God, to whom she had dedicated herself, quite as much as Enzio, to whom she is also dedicated. For him, despite everything, she will always remain "the little mirror," the "small light." At the beginning of the novel, when Enzio is waiting for Veronica at the foot of the stairs and sees her stopping, he asks her to come down, to come to him, "to bring light to the place where he is standing in the darkness."

Gertrud von Le Fort has succeeded in describing the presence of Christians in a world where there are unbelievers and even hate-filled unbelievers. We must suffer with others, for them and on account of them. Because Veronica agrees to suffer on account of Enzio, and to live this love that tears her apart and will bring her to the brink of death, she is always by his side in the love she experiences for him.

Unity is profoundly necessary because the love between two people, one of whom is a believer and the other an atheist, is here extraordinarily intense. It is a love which tears them apart and separates them from one another, but it flows out into something that is much broader than individual love, into a communion in charity and suffering. This is what Jeanette writes to her from Rome:

> A little while ago I wrote you that Don Angelo considers the situation in Western Christianity very serious. I often have the impression that for him all reality is plunged into the same dark night that has stricken his eyes. If I understand what he is saying, he considers apostasy [*Abfall*] so serious that it would be impossible to convert most men of our day. All we can do is save them by the love of reparation [*stellvertretende Liebe*].[72]

When the priest, Don Angelo, learns that Veronica's fiancé does not have the faith, his reaction is relayed to her by Jeanette:

> Your fiancé's lack of belief did not trouble him. It didn't even seem to surprise him. He seems to presuppose this lack

of belief in everyone. . . . You, he said, are on the only road
that is still open. Believers must enter into a total communion of love [*Liebesgemeinschaft*] with unbelievers. They
have to get out of their pious security [*frommen Sicherun-
gen*] and take on themselves the weight of their tragedy.
Then, they too will share their blessing [*Segen*].[73]

It would be wrong to conclude from these texts that we may
disregard the apostolic work of proclamation of the Word of
God. This is not what Gertrud von Le Fort means. She is
merely reminding us that unbelief in the West is so deeply
rooted, so mixed with resentment and ignorance, that it obliges
us to reflect upon the mystery of the division of the world
between believers and atheists. This is a new dimension of Western consciousness. If we do not place at the center of the apos-
tolate this repairing love which agrees to suffer for and with
others, any proclamation of the Gospel will be sterile.

The refore unity, a messianic promise, must be pursued with
hope. It is the unity of men in faith in God. But the present
situation shows us that this unity is not a human thing. There
is nothing facile about it. We have been and still are constantly
tempted to want to speed up the ways of salvation. We are constantly impelled to anticipate and to declare that the "Kingdom
is at hand." But political divisions as well as the split between
believers and non-believers teach us a prophetic truth: unity is,
above all, God's work. Only he can establish it, because only he
knows how many diversities compose it.

c) *Christian Unity*

The third form of division separates Christians, who ought to
be witnessing to unity in love, since they would be united in
one Church. Gertrud von Le Fort has not forgotten her Protestantism. She discovered in Catholicism the deepest riches of
the Lutheran pietism that her mother had given her. Obsessed
with Christian unity, Gertrud von Le Fort dedicated one of her
most beautiful novels to it: *Die magdeburgische Hochzeit* [The
marriage at Magdeburg].

The capture of Magdeburg in 1631 was one of the dramas of
the wars of religion. Beyond this crime of Christendom, we see

an eschatological hope of unity between separated Christians. We must live suffering this division, agreeing to suffer it, and agreeing not to rest until this scandalous wound has been healed.

> . . . It seems that the wall of the cathedral is shaking under the weight of a sin common to the faithful of both Churches, the immeasurable sin of forgetting what unites them. In the nave of the cathedral, Bake shows the great Christ above the rood-screen looking down at the triumphant Papists, with their drums and their trumpets, with the same unfathomable look of love and pain. . . . And everything then is changed. Where this atrocious crime of divided Christendom has just been perpetrated (the sack of Magdeburg which will forever separate hostile sisters), Magdeburg now appears to the Pastor as a Golgotha where all Christians will again become united.[74]

*   *   *

Gertrud von Le Fort's work is oriented around three poles: the Reich, the Church, and the Woman. This is why she wrote hymns to the Church. What can bring salvation to this world divided by hatred is the love which suffers in the place of others, and suffers with them.

This love is represented by the woman, the woman's veil, Veronica's veil on the face of Christ crucified. It is represented by the Church in her painful, torn, and broken love, for the Church suffers from the division that sets believers and unbelievers against one another. It also suffers from the fact that there is no way at present to unite all men in one City of Righteousness. *Opus justitiae pax* was the motto of Pius XII. *Pacem in terris*, said Pope John XXIII in his encyclical of Holy Thursday, 1963.

d) Rome and Jerusalem

Gertrud von Le Fort crowns her work with a feminine figure, that Rome in agony which we have already seen in Péguy. Veronica was converted at St. Peter's when she came upon the relics of the Passion one Holy Thursday.

For in those "seven stages of Rome" about which Victor Hugo speaks, there is the Rome of the Catacombs and the Rome of the churches. This modest and sorrowing Rome is that of the small basilicas but also the Rome of St. Peter's. Its cupola is built above the tomb of the Prince of the Apostles, who accepted the giving of his life as a witness to his faith. This also appears in another of her novels, *The Pope of the Ghetto,* in which she integrates into the problem of Christian disunity that of anti-Semitism, which shows the breadth of this work, one of the greatest of the twentieth century.

Beneath this sorrowing Rome there is the other image, the figure of Jerusalem. When we make our way to Christ's tomb, it is impossible to forget that it was here that Christ died that there might no longer be Jew or Gentile but one people, and yet at this very spot Christians are divided. They were so set against one another that they were unable to get along at all. It is a Moslem family that keeps the keys to the Basilica of the Holy Sepulcher.

Even at the place where Christ died that men might be one, they are split apart and divided among themselves. This image of Jerusalem is an image of the Church. It outlines the unity that was lost, is promised and on the way to be recovered, for Jerusalem is where Christ died and is risen.

> Urbs Jerusalem beata
> Dicta pacis visio
> Quae celsa de viventibus
> Saxis ad astra tolleris
> Et angelis coronata
> Ut sponsata comite . . .

NOTES TO CHAPTER 7

1. T. S. Eliot, *Collected Poems 1909–1935* (New York: Harcourt, 1934), p. 101.
2. T. S. Eliot, *Murder in the Cathedral* (New York: Harcourt, 1935), p. 13.
3. *Ibid.,* pp. 44–45.
4. *Ibid.,* pp. 47–50.

5. *Ibid.*, pp. 86–87.
6. T. S. Eliot, *The Cocktail Party* (New York: Harcourt, 1950), pp. 98–99.
7. *Ibid.*, p. 134.
8. *Ibid.*, pp. 137–138.
9. *Ibid.*, p. 132.
10. *Ibid.*, pp. 136–137.
11. *Ibid.*, p. 125.
12. *Ibid.*, pp. 139–140.
13. *Ibid.*, p. 125.
14. *Ibid.*, p. 128.
15. *Ibid.*, p. 154.
16. *Ibid.*, pp. 141–142.
17. *Ibid.*, p. 32.
18. *Ibid.*, p. 150.
19. *Ibid.*, p. 182.
20. *Ibid.*, p. 186.
21. *Ibid.*, p. 128.
22. T. S. Eliot, *The Elder Statesman* (New York: Farrar, Straus and Cudahy, 1959), p. 84.
23. *Ibid.*, p. 87.
24. *Ibid.*, pp. 101–102.
25. *Ibid.*, pp. 102–103.
26. *Ibid.*, p. 103.
27. *Ibid.*, p. 88.
28. *Ibid.*, pp. 104–105.
29. *Ibid.*, p. 105.
30. *Ibid.*, p. 110.
31. *Ibid.*, pp. 127–128.
32. *Ibid.*, p. 128.
33. Sigrid Undset, *The Wild Orchid* (New York: Knopf, 1932), pp. 192–193.
34. Undset, *The Burning Bush*, trans. Arthur G. Chater (New York: Knopf, 1932), pp. 35–36.
35. *The Wild Orchid*, p. 199.
36. *The Burning Bush*, pp. 412–413.
37. *Ibid.*, pp. 410–412.
38. *Ibid.*, pp. 415–416.
39. In the same fashion, a novel by William Barrett, called *The Left Hand of God*, presents characters that "cling" to their sin, while knowing they are sinners. This novel is the story of an

American aviator who has fallen into the hands of a brigand in China. He wants to return to the United States. In the meantime, a priest, sent to a mission some thirty miles away, dies. His replacement also dies, killed in an ambush. The American aviator takes the cassock of this priest and in clerical dress goes to the mission, where he will be able to get the first convoy going to the coast and from there embark for the United States.

When he reaches the mission he is received as a priest and is told that a Chinese who is going to die is waiting for the priest because he wants to go to confession. The aviator, caught in his game, does not know what to do. He does not dare say he is not a priest. He hears the Chinese's confession. Others are waiting by the confessional. He hears the confessions of these poor people. He is struck by what he has done. After a while he stops and puts his head in his hands. He had imagined that life was a kind of triumphal march of free-loaders passing beneath a series of triumphal arches and that one progressively arrived at one's goal through freedom of thought. He comes to the realization that this is not humanity at all. Humanity is the Chinese who confess their everyday sins, their sordid sins. They are attached to these sins, and yet he senses that they are ashamed and want to get rid of them, to confess them and ask forgiveness.

At this moment the aviator understands why he should have been a priest to give genuine absolution. He calls upon the Lord to arrange this. He rediscovers Christianity and the faith because he learns that men are not conquering heroes marching toward a "singing" future, but people who cling to their sins and who at the same time ask forgiveness for them from the Lord.

40. S. Undset, *Kristin Lavransdatter*, trans. Charles Archer (New York: Knopf, 1930), book 3, *The Cross*, pp. 1036–1037, 1038.

41. *Ibid.*, pp. 1040–1041.

42. S. Undset, *The Master of Hestviken*, trans. Arthur G. Chater (New York: Knopf, 1934), book 4, *The Son Avenger*, p. 338.

43. *Ibid.*, pp. 329–330.

44. Charles Péguy, *Oeuvres poétiques complètes* (Paris: Ed. La Pléidade, © Editions Gallimard, 1941), p. 178.

45. Charles Péguy, *Eve* (Paris: Ed. La Pléiade, © Editions Gallimard, 1941), pp. 707, 720, 708, 713–714.

46. *Ibid.*, p. 764.

47. *Ibid.*, pp. 750, 753, 758.

48. In Christ, the heir of Israel and the Roman Empire (the symbol of all civilizations), all who die for carnal earth also die for the beginning of the City of God. This is why a causative word appears in the text: The supernatural is itself carnal because, through the incarnation of the young and eternal God, it is present in time.

49. *Eve*, p. 843.

50. *Ibid.*, pp. 813–814.

51. Charles Péguy, *The Mystery of the Charity of Joan of Arc*, trans. Julian Green (New York: Pantheon, 1950), pp. 66–67.

52. *Eve*, pp. 938–940.

53. *Oeuvres poétiques complètes*, 1216, 1215, 1231.

54. Paul Claudel, *Tête d'Or*, trans. J. S. Newberry (New Haven: Yale, 1919), pp. 7–8.

55. *Ibid.*, pp. 70–71.

56. *Ibid.*, pp. 21–23.

57. *Ibid.*, pp. 169–170.

58. *Ibid.*, pp. 168–169.

59. Translator's note: The French word *aspirer* fits very well into the context, because it means both "to aspire" and "to breathe in." In addition there is an obvious assonance between the two words *espérer-aspirer*, adding to the poet's imagery.

60. This is quoted from Paul-André Lesort, *Paul Claudel par lui-même*, (Paris: Ed. du Seuil, 1963), p. 26.

61. A Blanchet, *La Littérature et le Spirituel*, I (Paris: Aubier, 1960).

62. *P.-A. Lesort*, p. 28.

63. *Ibid.*, p. 54.

64. Paul Claudel, *The Satin Slipper*, trans. Rev. John O'Connor (New Haven: Yale University Press, 1931), pp. 179–180.

65. *Ibid.*, p. 300.

66. Gertrud von Le Fort, *Der Kranz der Engel*, (Munich: Ehrenwirth, 1953), pp. 214–215. English translation after Moeller.

67. *Ibid.*, p. 197.

68. *Ibid.*, pp. 22–23.

69. *Ibid.*, p. 222.

70. *Ibid.*, p. 273.

71. *Ibid.*, p. 272.

72. *Ibid.*, p. 23.

73. *Ibid.*, p. 133.

74. Gertrud von Le Fort, *Die magdeburgische Hochzeit* (Leipzig: Insel-Verlag, 1938), pp. 238–239. English translation after the French edition: *Les Noces de Magdebourg* (Paris: Ed. du Seuil, 1954), p. 187.

Conclusion

SALVATION IS LIFE, THAT IS, JUSTICE AND LOVE. IT IS MEN'S BOND among themselves in unity. It is a work in common. In the film *Hiroshima mon amour*, from their hotel room every morning the lovers hear a man passing under their window and coughing. A personal happiness that was not open to this window at Hiroshima would be sterile. We are together for better or worse. We are bound to the earth. It is the place of our incarnation, and salvation can only be justice and love on this earth.

This earth? Believers know that for it to become the place of the coming of the Kingdom, it must be transfigured and become "a new heaven and a new earth" (Isa. 66:22; Rom. 8:18–22). Non-believers fear that in this transfiguration there is a kind of sleight-of-hand, a mystification, that makes one forget the earth of men. But Jesus is salvation because he is the Savior. In the last analysis, salvation is not an abstract notion, but a person, the person of the Incarnate Word, Jesus, whose name means "Savior."

Abstract statements have never moved anyone. The proclamation of the good news, which *is* Jesus Christ, can touch the heart.

But who knows Jesus Christ? People write books to speak about Christianity. This short book has been written to give a few signposts of salvation. As we conclude, we discover that we have hardly spoken of Jesus at all. He is "the leader who would take them to their salvation" (Heb. 2:10). There is salvation in none other than Jesus Christ (Acts 4:12). He is our hope, our patient expectation. He also gives us the strength of this hope and is the one who makes us listen joyfully to these words of St. Paul, read by a television commentator at the beginning of Paul VI's pilgrimage to the Holy Land: "For salvation is nearer to us now than when we first believed; the night is far gone, the day is at hand" (Rom. 13:11–12).

"Watchman, what of the night?" sang the evangelist of the Old Testament, Isaiah. "And you, child, will be called the prophet of the Most High; for you will go before the Lord to prepare his ways, to give knowledge of salvation to his people in the forgiveness of their sins;" these words of Zechariah in St. Luke, "the scribe of the gentleness of Christ," I make my own. For my only wish is that a few of the writers mentioned in this essay may be, for just one reader, a John the Baptist, "giving to the people the knowledge of salvation."

Index

Acquainted With the Night, 6
Action, L', 69
Adulterous Woman, The, 30
A la trace de Dieu, 35
Amers, 93
Anabasis, 87, 165
Anouilh, Jean, 118
Arbre, L', 164
Aristotle, 23

Balzac, Honoré de, 99
Baring, Maurice, 139
Barrès, Auguste M., 99
Beauvoir, Simone de, 21, 24, 28, 29, 42, 44, 127
Becket, 118
Bergman, Ingmar, 142
Bergson, Henri, 35, 75, 145
Bernanos, Georges, 97, 99–100, 110, 116
Blanchet, A., 97, 168
Blondel, Maurice, 69
Böll, Heinrich, 6
Book of Revelation, 71
Bossuet, Jacques Bénigne, 25
Bourget, Charles J., 99
Break of Noon, 169

Brecht, Bertolt, 23, 24
Brunschvicg, Léon, 32
Burning Bush, The, 140

Cahiers de la Quinzaine, 153
Camus, Albert, 25, 26, 28, 30, 31, 36, 48, 49, 50, 52, 53, 57, 59, 84, 111
Cas François Sagan, Le, 48
Castle, The, 58
Césaire, Aimé, 82
Chronique, 93
Cicero, 3
Claudel, Paul, 82, 118, 161, 162, 163, 165, 166, 167, 168, 169, 172, 173
Cocktail Party, The, 123, 124, 127
Condemned of Altona, The, 41, 52, 132, 133, 134
Croisade, La, 26

Daphne Adeane, 139
Delaporte, Louis Joseph, 153
Delavigne, Casimir, 56
Demons, The, 49
Diary of a Country Priest, 99, 110, 116
Die magdeburgische Hochzeit, 178

187

Discours sur l'histoire universelle, 25
Dostoyevsky, Fëdor, 49, 116
Du Bos, Charles, 4, 134
Duhamel, Georges, 52
Duras, Marguerite, 36, 44

Each in His Darkness, 105
Elder Statesman, The, 132, 136
Eliot, T. S., 118, 123, 124, 125, 131, 132, 136, 138, 139, 140
Eloges and Other Poems, 83, 84, 85–87
Esprit et l'Eau, L', 172
Eve, 152, 156, 158, 160
Exile and the Kingdom, The, 50

Fall, The, 50, 143
Family Reunion, The, 124
Fanon, Frantz, 82
Faulkner, William, 28, 49, 53
Fluchère, Henry, 132
Force of Circumstance, The, 29
Foucauld, Charles de, 48

Gandhi, Mahatma, 48
Genêt, Jean, 68
Greene, Graham, 97, 100, 116
Green, Julian, 12, 51, 97, 99, 104, 105, 110, 116
Grousset, René, 26
Guersant, Marcel, 44
Guillemin, Henri, 152
Gymnadenia, 140, 142

Heart of the Matter, The, 97
Hegel, Georg Wilhelm, 14, 69
Hiroshima mon amour, 36, 37, 131
Hollow Men, The, 118
Hourdin, George, 48
Hugo, Victor, 104, 180

Jammes, Francis, 82
Jean Barois, 32–34
Jean-Paul, 44

Kafka, Franz, 57, 58, 59, 60, 66, 126, 127, 173

Kant, Immanuel, 14, 28
Keats, John, 5
Kierkegaard, Sören, 59
King Lear, 136
Kristin Lavransdatter, 146

Le Fort, Gertrud von, 11, 118, 172, 173, 174, 177, 178, 179, 180
Lenin, Nikolai, 48
Lesort, Paul André, 169
Lubac, Henri de, 23
Lyonnais Club, The, 52

Malraux, André, 57
Mandarins, The, 29
Marcel, Gabriel, 35, 64, 123, 129, 136
Marriage at Magdeburg, The, 178
Martin du Gard, Roger, 32
Marx, Karl, 14
Master of Hestviken, The, 146, 148
Mauriac, François, 97, 98, 99, 100, 104, 116
Memoirs of a Dutiful Daughter, 21
Montherlant, Henry de, 46
Mother, The, 23, 24
Mother Courage, 23
Murder in the Cathedral, 118, 119, 124
Mystère des Saints Innocents, Le, 158
Mystery of the Charity of Joan of Arc, The, 157

No Exit, 36, 132

Oedipus at Colonus, 136
Oedipus Rex, 134
Olav Audunssön, 146, 148
Ouragan sur le sucre, 20

Pacem in Terris, 11, 23
Pascal, Blaise, 11
Péguy, Charles, 4, 54, 104, 118, 151, 152, 153, 154, 158, 160, 173, 179

Perse, St.-John, 81–96, 132, 165
Picture of Dorian Gray, 139
Plague, The, 31, 111
Politique tirée de l'Ecriture Sainte, 25
Pope of the Ghetto, The, 180
Port-Royal, 46
Possessed, The, 49
Prime of Life, The, 29
Prophète Péguy, Le, 153
Proudhon et le Catholicisme, 23
Proust, Marcel, 85

Que sais-je?, 26
Qu'est-ce que la Litterature?, 4

Rabemananjara, 82
Rebel, The, 25
Remembrance of Things Past, 85
Requiem for a Nun, 49
Rerum Novarum, 23, 24
Rimbaud, Arthur, 36
Rivière, Jacques, 35
Roman Fountain, The, 174
Rome n'est plus dans Rome, 64
Rousseaux, André, 3, 93, 153

Sagan, Françoise, 10, 48
Sartre, Jean Paul, 5, 20, 21, 28, 36, 39, 40, 42, 50, 54, 56, 57, 67, 68, 127, 132, 175
Satin Slipper, The, 168, 170, 171
Seamarks, 93

Second Sex, The, 42
Senghor, Léopold, 82
Schwob, René, 53
Shakespeare, William, 123, 136
Song of Songs, 71
Sophocles, 136
Spaak, Henri, 19
Strange River, 51
Summer Games, 142

Teilhard de Chardin, Pierre, 10, 11, 81
Tete d'Or, 161, 163, 164, 165, 169
Tidings Brought to Mary, The, 172
Trial, The, 58

Unamuno, Miguel de, 35
Under the Sun of Satan, 116
Undset, Sigrid, 140, 142, 146

Valéry, Paul, 13, 44, 89, 174
Veil of Veronica, The, 173
Very Easy Death, A, 29
Vipers' Tangle, 98, 100–104
Voltaire, 82

Warren, Robert Penn, 28
Weil, Simone, 18
Wilde, Oscar, 139
Wild Orchid, The, 140
Wilhelm Meister, 140
Winds, 88, 89, 94
Words, The, 68
Wreath of Angels, The, 174